Bruce: A Chronicle Play by John Davidson

John Davidson was born at Barrhead, East Renfrewshire on 11th April 1857.

In 1862 his family moved to Greenock and there he began his education at Highlanders' Academy. Davidson would now spend many years at school and the beginnings of a career in various industries before gaining employment in various schools.

By now literature was a large part of his activities and his first published work was 'Bruce, A Chronicle Play' in 1886. Four other plays quickly followed including the somewhat brilliant pantomimic 'Scaramouch in Naxos' (1889).

With his reputation gradually providing an income he was also able to explore his true medium; Verse. 'In a Music Hall and Other Poems' (1891) together with 'Fleet Street Eclogues' (1893) were ample proof that he possessed a quite rare, genuine and distinctive poetic gift.

Davidson now turned further and further towards verse. In 1894 he published his most popular volume, 'Ballads and Songs' (1894), and this was followed by a further 'Fleet Street Eclogues' (Second Series) (1896) and by 'New Ballads' (1897) and 'The Last Ballad' (1899).

As the new century dawned Davidson was hard at work on a series of 'Testaments', in which he gave definite expression to his philosophy and were published over a seven year period; 'The Testament of a Vivisector' (1901), 'The Testament of a Man Forbid' (1901), 'The Testament of an Empire Builder' (1902), and 'The Testament of John Davidson' (1908).

However, on 23rd March 1909, with his finances in ruins, the onset of cancer and profound hopelessness and clinical depression he left his house for the last time. His body was only found on September 18th by some local fishermen.

Index of Contents

DRAMATIS PERSONS

Robert Bruce, Earl of Carrich, afterwards King of Scotland
Edward Bruce
Nigel Bruce
Lamberton, Archbishop of St. Andrews
Walter, the Steward of Scotland
Sir William Wallace
Sir James Douglas
Sir Thomas Randolf
Sir Christopher Seton
Sir John Seton
James Crombe
Kirkpatrick
Comyn, Earl of Badenoch
Comyn, Earl of Buchan
Macduff, Earl of Fife
Sir Robert Comyn
Edward I., King of England
Edward II., King of England
The Earl of Pembroke
Lord Henry Percy
Lord Robert Clifford
Sir Ingram de Umfraville
Sir Giles de Argentine
Sir Peter Mallorie, Justiciary of England
Hugh Beaumont
Isabella, Countess of Carrick, afterwards Queen of Scotland.
Isobel, Countess of Buchan
Countess of Badenoch.
Lady Douglas.
An Old Man, a Young Friar, a Messenger, a Forester, a Spy.
Lords, Ladies, Gentlemen, Monks, Soldiers, &c.

BRUCE

ACT I

SCENE I.—London. A Room in the Palace

KING EDWARD I, **EARL OF PEMBROKE**, **LORD HENRY PERCY** and **LORD ROBERT CLIFFORD**.

EDWARD I
Once more, my lords, the rude north claims our care.
A faction there is still opposed to peace,
Strongly ill-willed to England and to me,
Obdurate, set, incorrigibly wroth—
A band whose blood is of the liquid flame
That often madly jets in savage veins,
When wisdom would bestow some blessed gift,
Some pearl which ignorance rejects with scorn,
And chafes and frets and sets the world on fire.
The Bruce, my lords, has fled the English Court:
He goes to Scotland, and his guiding star
Is that same beacon of rebellious light
Built up by every burning Scottish heart.
Astonishment and curiosity
Shoulder each other in your crowded eyes
Like townsmen gazing from a window's height
At some strange pageantry afoot below;
There let them crowd, for wonders are to pass.
Were I to ask you, now, if Bruce or Comyn
Has played the fairer game, you might say this:
They cannot be compared—Bruce always with,
And Comyn always opposite to me;
Yet have they both held by the cause they chose:
So there's a parity of constancy.
Such answer might be yours. Then I would say,
They both are faithless: here I hold the proof.

[Exhibits a scroll.

This is a deed transferring Bruce's lands
To Comyn, who exchanges for the same
His claim—it's written so—to Scotland's crown.
He promises besides to aid the Bruce
To gain the state and name of King of Scots.

There are their signatures.

PEMBROKE
By miracle—
Or how did this indenture reach your hands?

EDWARD I
John Comyn sent it me. You see—base rogues!—Bruce false
to me, and Comyn false to Bruce.

PEMBROKE
My liege, Bruce hitherto has borne a name
As bright and glorious as his golden shield,
Untarnished by dishonour's rusty breath.
This paper may be forged.

EDWARD I
That was my thought;
And so I had a copy of it made,
And sent to Bruce last night. My messenger
Asked, being charged so far, some word from him.
He half denied; but compromised, and craved
Three days to answer. So much grace I gave.
This is the first day, and last night he fled.

PEMBROKE
A sign of guilt. What will your Highness do?

EDWARD I
With your good counsel, lords, doubtless the best!

PERCY
To horse, and take the knave alive or dead!

EDWARD I
A speedy finish; but consider this:
Comyn and Bruce divide the land of Scots;
They now are mortal foes; why need we stir
To fight two cocks who will each other slay
Between the high walls of their Scottish pit?
Yet Pembroke, Clifford, and bold Harry Percy
Be ready at a word to lead your knights
Across the border.

PERCY
Nor can that summons come
Too soon for us.

EDWARD I

I would your willing haste
Were from the proof removed a farther cast:
And so were Wallace wise as he is wight
It would be. Twice I offered grace and love,
If he would govern Scotland in my name.
He thanked me for my grace and for my love,
But at my terms he laughed as at a jest.
Had he accepted them, I say again,
As there is none so fit to rule the Scots,
Your willing service had been hardly asked.

PERCY

Let me say this: had such a league been struck
Between your Highness and the valiant Scot,
You might have borne your banners through the world.

PEMBROKE

What specious arguments could Wallace urge?

EDWARD I

O, ask me not! My patience served me ill
To hear him out. How can I then rehearse
His saucy reasons, wasting breath and wrath!
Within short space you all shall hear himself;
A fortnight hence, I think, he will be tried.
And now, Lord Clifford, James of Douglas comes
To claim his father's lands, which you possess.
Tell me, who knows, what kind of man he is,
That we may judge how he will bear himself?

CLIFFORD

A man of men, although my mortal foe.
I knew him well in Paris ere these broils.
Unarmed, a gentle blitheness graced his style:
A dainty lisp engaged his auditors
With tickling pleasure; such a piquant touch
Was in the Scottish Hector, as they called him,
Tripping with helpless tongue, like rose-lipped girls.
But when he armed his body, then his soul
Was harnessed in a dress of adamant.
In council-halls, o'er ladies' lutes, in war,
Brave, courteous, wise, loyal to truth, he was:
So is he: Douglas changes but for good.

EDWARD I

You praise him highly. You shall answer him.
He comes. Make room.

[Enter **SIR JAMES DOUGLAS**.

We know your errand, sir.
Speak, and Clifford here will answer you.

DOUGLAS
Lord Clifford will, and must: be sure of that.
I also crave King Edward's open ear.
Clifford will reckon with me for my land:
You, sire, must render an account of blood.

CLIFFORD
Clifford has yet to learn why Douglas dare
Speak such a swift defiance.

EDWARD I [Turning his back to **DOUGLAS**]
Answer him
On this wise, my good lord:—Your father, sir,
A faithless felon, died a prisoner
In Edward's dungeon; and his forfeit lands
Reverted to the crown. It pleased the king
To make me lord of Douglasdale. Go, then,
Buy land where'er you may, I keep my own.
He has his answer, follow me, my lords.

[**EDWARD I**, **PEMBROKE**, **CLIFFORD**, and **PERCY** go out.

DOUGLAS
There's justice in the heavens if not in kings!
He might have listened. It is very plain
King Edward means to play the tyrant now.
Yet tyrants can be courteous. Insolent!
To toss an answer o'er his shoulder at me,
Whetting with crude affront, the pointed "No,"
As one would check a cringeing beggar's plea.
One way is left, a flinty, narrow way,
The rebel's way, the way I still have shunned:
And yet it seems a broad, green, garden-walk,
Since I elect to be a traveller there.
Now though it be as hopeless as to stem
The Solway's tide, or toss the deep-based Bass
From Forth to France, with all my strength I'll fight
Against this tyrannous usurping king.
How strange that I should find rebellion's storm
The happy haven where my troubles end!
But so it is: my cares are blown away;
Light-hearted vigour is my lot once more;

And trampled conscience, like the heath released,
Springs up, and breathes sweet scent of approbation.

[Goes out.

SCENE II.—Dumfries. The Greyfriars Church

Enter **BRUCE** and **COMYN OF BADENOCH**.

COMYN
I thought you were in London, cousin mine.

BRUCE
And still would have me there, or anywhere,
But by your side.

COMYN
Why is your tongue so harsh,
Your eye so big, your face so dimmed with ire?

BRUCE
Why falter you? Why has your colour fled?
Why, but because my tongue still speaks its thought;
Because my face wears not the darker show
Of death's grimace upon a spear's long neck,
Grotesquely ornamenting London Bridge;
Because my limbs are not the bait of crows,
The gazing-stock of crowds in Scotland's towns;
Because I live and am at liberty:
These are the reasons why you tremble now.

COMYN
Not so; it is because I think you mad:
These monstrous breathings are insanity:
You shake with passion, hissing out your words.
I fear you; and I will have witnesses
Or no more conference.

[Going.

BRUCE [Seizing his arm]
With honest men
God is sufficient witness. Are you true?
You know my ground of wrath as well as I.

COMYN

Your words are like your brow, darker than night.

BRUCE
Be this the sun that shall illumine them.

[Exhibits a scroll.

Sun, said I! rather inky light of hell,
Whereby you may behold your treachery.
I see it's true what I have heard of men,
Who, knowing right, pursue a wrongful course:
Custom uprears athwart the source of shame
A fragile dam; but when another marks
The waves that beat behind, they swell and burst
The sandy sea-wall of hypocrisy,
Like a packed gulf delivered by the moon.
That flood is in your face: you blush like fire.

COMYN
I blush to be accused of this great wrong.

BRUCE
Comyn, you lie. Look, see, the very words
Of that compact, which we with aching hearts
Drew up and signed and swore in Stirling town.
Have you forgotten how we wept hot tears
Condoling over Scotland's misery?
Its fertile plains, that richer were than gold,
Burnt up with fire, salted with tears and blood;
Its cots and palaces confounded low
In stony litters that the soil reclaims;
Its wealthy towns and pleasant places sacked;
Its people?—Ah! we could not sound our grief
For wives made widows; husbands, left alone;
And children, blighted by too early bareness
Of parents' comfortable snowy wisdom:
Death and destruction feasting everywhere.
We found ourselves to blame; therefore we wept,
Repenting of our jealousy and strife.
This pact united us in sacred bonds
For ever to oppose the English rule.
We prayed that our conjunction, like two stars
Meeting auspiciously for Scotland's weal,
Might yield its war-worn people prosperous peace;
And o'er the border cast calamities
Of such deserved and overwhelming woe,
That England never more should be inclined,
Nor have the power to wage a conquering war.

We then embraced, and you with trembling breath
Thanked God that Bruce and Comyn now were friends.
Two copies of our compact we endorsed.
Here is a third that's neither yours nor mine:
King Edward sent it me; whence had he it?

COMYN

Unless King Edward sent it back to you,
You having given it him, I cannot tell.

BRUCE

God keep my hands from blood! O soulless wretch!
Obtuse, unthinking liar! Could I note
The shape of good that dances in your brain
To be matured for service by denial,
Perhaps that might extenuate your lie.
But knowing nothing save your treachery,
And hardened daring of a damning fact,
Relentless hate expels all dreams of love
That harboured once toward you within my heart.

COMYN

If, then, your rage is for the present spent,
A few plain words may hope for audience.
What proof have you that Edward had this writ
Through me or mine? Impartial sense would blame,
Not me, who ever have been Scotland's friend,
And foremost in opposing Edward's power,
But you, the truckling lord, inheriting
And practising your father's policy,
Which was to follow at the Longshanks' heel,
And fawn for smiles, and wait his Highness' whim
To pay the lacqueying with a dirty crown.

BRUCE

This idle mockery becomes you well.
Did any doubt remain of your dark sin,
The hunting out a mote within my eye
To poise the beam that does disfigure yours,
Would make me sure.

COMYN

What legal proof, I say?

BRUCE

The laws of God, honour and loyalty
Condemn you traitor to their interests.
I judge you guilty, for I know right well

King Edward never had this scroll from me,
And no one else could give it him but you.
Your heart condemns you, though you brave it thus.

COMYN
And yet I say again, I swear by Heaven,
I never saw that paper till to-day.

BRUCE
Talk not of seeing!—Come to the altar here.

[They advance to the altar.

Now lay your hand upon the traitorous sheet,
Call God to witness that you speak the truth,
And swear once more you have not broken faith.
Beneath your feet the dust of true men rests,
Your ancestors and mine; this lofty roof,
These consecrated walls and columns high
Are wont to hear the sounds of sacred song,
The gospel of the holy Christ of God;
This is God's house; this altar is God's throne.
Now, can you swear? You will not do it, sure.

COMYN
And what shall hinder me while I have breath?
Without my instigation or connivance
Our compact reached the King. If God's in heaven,
And I speak false, may I this moment die.

BRUCE [Stabbing **COMYN**, who falls]
God is in heaven, and my hand wields his wrath! . . . .
What have I done? A madman's dreadful deed!
I was engulfed, and now I'm cast ashore.
O, in our passionless, reflective hours
We lock emotion in a glass-walled jail
Of crisp philosophy; or give it scope
As far as prudence may enlarge its steps!
But to some sense a small distraction comes—
Across the sight a butterfly, a flower—
The fetters snap, the prison crumbles—off!—
To clasp the air where shone our will-o-wisp!
For no gewgaw have I burst reason's bonds,
But to avenge a gross iniquity
That clamoured brazenly to heaven and earth.
O, it was human!—It was devilish!
Here on the altar—O, the sacrilege!
That man of my own blood, whom I adjured,

By every holy thing, to speak no wrong,
I do wrong, slaying. O, heinous sacrilege!—
Perhaps he is not dead. Comyn, look up;
Speak; make some sign. Alas! that fatal blow
Was aimed too surely at my cousin's heart!
I used God's name too when I struck him dead!
O horrid blasphemy! The sacrilege!

[Going.

[Enter **KIRKPATRICK**.

KIRKPATRICK
My Lord!

BRUCE
I fear I have slain Comyn.

[Goes out.

KIRKPATRICK
Ha!
You fear!—Then I'll make sure. He opes his eyes.

COMYN
False—foolish—dying—guilty—perjured—lost!

[Dies.

KIRKPATRICK [Stabbing **COMYN**]
Something to staunch your muttering. No fear, now.

[Enter **SIR ROBERT COMYN** with his sword drawn.

ROBERT COMYN
Stop villain! Hold your hand, rash murderer!

KIRKPATRICK
I only gave a grace-thrust to your nephew
To end his agony. Put up your sword.
He died a good death on the altar-steps.

ROBERT COMYN
Kirkpatrick, you have aided in a deed,
Unseconded, even in these fearful times.

KIRKPATRICK
Strong words and stiffly spoken. Does your sword

Keep pace with your sharp tongue?

ROBERT COMYN
We'll try.

KIRKPATRICK
Come on!

[They fight, and **ROBERT COMYN** falls.

ROBERT COMYN
Is this the day of judgment for our house?
Kinsman, I was your follower on earth,
And now I am your henchman through death's vale.

[Dies.

[Enter **EDWARD BRUCE**, **SIR CHRISTOPHER** and **SIR JOHN SETON**, and other **GENTLEMEN**.

SIR CHRISTOPHER SETON
Two Comyns dead! Bruce only spoke of one.

KIRKPATRICK
I slew the other. He would have me fight.

SIR JOHN SETON
Alas! and could it be no other way?
There was enough dissension in the realm
Without a feud between these families,
Highest in state and strongest in the field.

1st GENTLEMAN
Comyn is dead, and Bruce has laid him low.
The dead may slay the living. What say you?

2nd GENTLEMAN
I say so too. The stroke that Comyn killed
May yet recoil upon his murderer.

EDWARD BRUCE
Judge not, my friends. A murder has been done
With outward signs of most unrighteous wrath.
But think who did the deed—the noblest Scot,
The knightliest chevalier, the kindliest friend,
The prince of brothers. I, who know, say this.
The very horror and the sacrilege
That frame the crime with dreader circumstance,
Cry out the doer was insane the while,

And recommend him to your lenience.
Therefore, take warning; and before you judge
Let your bloods cool, lest you be guilty too
Of foolish rashness in your condemnation.
My brother left a message for you all:
He asks you who are friends to visit him
to-morrow at Lochmaben; where he means
To lay the matter of his crime before you,
And take your counsel on the consequence.

1st GENTLEMAN
It's fair we should withhold our judgment, sirs,
Until we be possessed of this event,
The cause and manner of its happening.

[Shouting within.

[Enter **NIGEL BRUCE**.

NIGEL BRUCE
The people buzz and clamour to be led.
The news of Comyn's death has made them mad;
If blood were wine, and they had drunk of it
To fulness, they could not be more mature
For any mischief that the time suggests.

EDWARD BRUCE
Good mischief, if the English suffer it.
I'll be their captain. Caesar pricked his horse
Across the Rubicon, defying Rome.
Bruce pricked John Comyn over death's dark stream,
Defying England. Caesar triumphed: Bruce
Shall triumph too. And now begins the fight.

[All go out.

SCENE III.—The Same

MONKS enter and lay the **BODIES** side by side. A bell tolls, and the **MONKS** kneel round the altar. Then enter the **COUNTESS OF BADENOCH**, and **COMYN, EARL OF BUCHAN**, and the **COUNTESS OF BUCHAN**

BUCHAN
You holy men, give place a little while.

A MONK
To whom?

BUCHAN
The wife and friends of slaughtered Comyn.

[The **MONKS** retire.

COUNTESS OF BADENOCH
Would any mortal think to look at me
This dead man was my husband? Should I weep,
And rend with sighs my breast, and wring my hands;
Peal out my sorrow, like a vesper bell
Calling the cloistered echo's shadowy choir
To take the burden of a woeful dirge;
Enrobe myself in that dishevelment
Which tyrannous grief compels his subjects pale
To show their vassalage by putting on,
I might persuade myself and you, my friends,
That I am sorry for my husband's death:
Even as an actor, lacking any cue,
Visible, tangible, as I have here,
Steps lightly at a word upon the stage,
Leaving his brothers and their merry chat,
And takes upon him any passion's show
With such devotion and abandonment,
That what was first a cloak becomes a soul,
And audience and actor both are held
Dissolved in ecstasy; which, breaking, back
From high heroics to sad homeliness
Their spirits are precipitated straight.
But I'll not play the broken heart, for you,
My friends, my audience, know the cause I have
Rather to laugh than weep. O wretched corpse!
What habitation holds the spirit now
Which Bruce ejected rashly, warrantless,
Pulling the house about the tenant's ears?

BUCHAN
He loved me little, and he loved you less;
And by his death he leaves a legacy,
The taking up of which, if spirits watch
From where eternally they rest or pine,
Our tragic, many-scened mortality,
Will reconcile him to his sudden death.

COUNTESS OF BUCHAN
Husband, what legacy?

BUCHAN

A mortal feud.

COUNTESS OF BUCHAN
Will you avenge on Bruce the death of him
Whom his best friends lament not?

BUCHAN
Yes, I must.
And good Sir Robert, too—his blood cries out.
It is a duty that the world will look
To see performed directly and with speed,
Admitting no perfunct, half-passive dance
On patient Providence. Dissuade me not,
For it becomes you not. There is a thing
That vaguely circulates in certain spheres
Concerning you, my dearest. Sad am I
That from my lips it first should taint your ears;
But you must know it now. Give me your hand.
This white and fragrant palm from guilty deeds,
That harden more than penitential toil,
Or from the touch of slime, is not more free,
Than your unshriven soul from infant thoughts
Swaddled in shame. But foul-tongued calumny,
Tutored by hatred, like a jabbering bird
With implication lewd repeats your name
And Bruce's in a breath.

COUNTESS OF BUCHAN
Alas, I know!
The lying scandal that benights my life
Will be a foil to make my memory shine.—
If it confronts you graven on the sky
To visit retribution on his head
Whose hand laid low your cousin's, be it so:
I'll not invade your secrets; but I mean
To do what woman can for Bruce's cause,
Which whispers tell me will be Scotland's soon.

BUCHAN
Well, we'll not quarrel. We'll talk of this again.

COUNTESS OF BADENOCH
Come take me home. I'm in a gentler mood.
Let those good cowls return and pray their best.

[The **COUNTESS OF BADENOCH** and the **EARL** and **COUNTESS OF BUCHAN** go out. The **MONKS** advance and kneel, and the scene closes.

ACT II

SCENE I.—Lochmaben. A Room in the Castle

Enter **LAMBERTON, ARCHBISHOP OF ST ANDREWS, EDWARD** and **NIGEL BRUCE**, the **TWO SETONS, SIR THOMAS RANDOLF**, and other **LORDS** and **GENTLEMEN**.

LAMBERTON
My lords and gentlemen, this is no time
For ceremony, which, when lazy peace
Has rusted o'er the world's slack businesses,
Oils easily the motion of affairs;
For now events impel each other on,
And higher powers than beadles usher them.
I am commissioned by the noble Bruce
To greet you heartily and wish you well
While you remain within Lochmaben's walls.
By my advice he begs you to excuse
His absence, while I speak. When you have heard
I doubt not that you will. He has confessed
The sacrilegious crime of yesterday,
Contritely and with simple truthfulness.
No exculpation, no defence at all,
Such as we know there is, he offered me.
Some of us here may hold that Bruce's act
Should rather be extolled than stigmatised.
We know for certain now what was the wrong
That Comyn, having wrought, denied on oath,
And all our sympathy goes out to Bruce.
But such the old deceitfulness of sin
That feelings of the sweetest comfort oft
Mislead us to embrace iniquity.
Man's worst of deeds God turns to good account:
A penance, which I hope will work God's will,
I have enjoined on the humiliate earl.
I mean to crown him, Robert, King of Scots:
His task will be to make that title good.
Now I have said a word that stirs your blood,
Begetting hope and courage, valiant twins.
And yet it is not I that speak, but God:
Surely God speaks. The sequence of events,
Of which this conference is the latest bud,
Appears to me a heavenly oracle,
As evident as Aaron's sprouting rod,
Commanding Robert Bruce to be the king.

He would have placed the crown on Comyn's head
Had Comyn wished, that Scotland might be one;
But Comyn thought to get the crown by guile,
And like an impious fool betrayed his friend,
Setting between him and the English king
A gulf of enmity impassable.
Edward will judge him out of church and law;
But in our Scotch communion he is safe:
And being out of law, there is no way,
Except to be our king, above the law.
Needs must, my lords; and is not need God's will?

EDWARD BRUCE
It is the will of God.

ALL
Bruce shall be king.

[Enter **BRUCE**.

Long live the King! Long live King Robert Bruce!

BRUCE
You hail me by a name that may be mine
In more than word, but not without your aid.
There are not many Scots besides yourselves
Who will acknowledge me their King. Think well
Before you pledge your faith to one outlawed;
For so I am, if law depend on power.
Scotland, the Isles, and England are my foes:
My friends are individual; on my hands
They may be counted. Lennox, Athole, Cairns,
Fleming, the Hayes, the Frasers, Sommerville,
Glasgow, and Moray, sum the list with you:
These only are the Scots whom I may rule.

SIR CHRISTOPHER SETON
Then only these deserve the name of Scot.

LAMBERTON
Right, Seton!

RANDOLF
We are Scots, the rest are slaves!
Freeman and Scot have ever meant the same.

LAMBERTON
Carrick or King?

BRUCE
King, by God's will and yours.

LAMBERTON
Sometimes we please ourselves with images
Of deeds heroic. The unstabled thought,
Enfranchised by rough-riding passion, winds
A haughty course and laughs at depth and height:
But the blood tires; and lo! our thought, a steed,
That from his rider ever takes the mood,
Pants, droops, turns tail, and hobbles home to stall.
Look in yourselves, and see if vain conceit
Or lofty daring, lord it o'er your minds.
This thing is sure: reason must be constrained:
You must be hot, believing, fanatic;
You must be wrathful, patriotic, rash;
Forethought abandon o'er to providence;
Let prudence lag behind you, like a snail,
Bearing its house with care upon its back;
Take counsel only of the circumstance
That shapes itself in doing of the deed;
Be happy, scornful, death-defiant: strong
You will be then matchless, invincible.
What! shall we go to Scone, and crown Bruce king?

RANDOLF
At once, Lord Archbishop.

SIR JOHN SETON
To Glasgow, first,
To take our friends there with us.

LAMBERTON
That is best.
Is it your will to be crowned king at Scone?

BRUCE
Most reverend father, and my noble friends,
If language were to me in place of thought,
I could pour grateful speeches in your ears;
But words are wanting. I am helpless, dumb;
I would be lonely; I would think awhile.

LAMBERTON
Think worthy thoughts, that only second are
To worthy deeds; yet their begetters too.
We'll leave you till our little troop's arrayed.

BRUCE
You are very kind, my lords.

[All go out except **BRUCE**.

I'm not a man
Much given to meditate. When pending thoughts
Hurtle each other in the intellect,
Darkening that firmament like thunder-clouds,
To let them lighten forth in utterance
Clears up the sky, confused with swaying rack.
My life begins a new departure here;
And like one dying all my time appears
Even on the instant, in eternal light.
Ambition struck the hours that measured it.
My pact with Comyn was half-hearted. What!
The passion that laid hold upon my soul
When he was killed—When he was killed? I think
I'm to myself too merciful; but yet
I seemed to do some bidding:—were there not
Alloys of gladness that the bond was loosed,
Of jealousy that Comyn barred my way,
Mixed in the blow that paid the traitor's wage?
There are two voices whispering in my ear:
This is the bane of self-communion. Now,
Right in thy teeth, or in thy toothless chaps,
I swear, antiquity, first thoughts are best:
Their treble notes I still shall hearken to,
And let no second, murmuring soft, seduce
Their clear and forthright meaning. It is gone,
The flash of revelation: dallying does
With intuition as with other chance.
I would to God that I might ever hear
The trump of doom pealing along the sky,
And know that every common neighbour day
Is the last day, and so live on and fight
In presence of the judgment. Wishing this
Have I not broached the very heart of truth?
Each unmarked moment is an end of time,
And this begins the future.

[Enter **ISABELLA**.

Isabella!

ISABELLA
What in this time of doleful accidents

Could move the joyful shouts I heard just now?

BRUCE
My dearest, what would make you shout for joy?

ISABELLA
I have not shouted since I was a girl;
But now, I think, if any happy thing
Should spring into my life, I would cry out,
I have been so unhappy, and so long.
Tell me you'll never leave me any more;
Then will I cry, and weep, for very joy.

BRUCE
Heaven grant it may be so!

ISABELLA
If there is hope!—
Did I not shout now?—I will nurse it warm,
And pet it like a darling, till it come
To be what I imagine in the fact,
Or in the fancy; for I will go mad:
I'll bend myself to lose all faculty,
All thought, remembrance, all intelligence,
So to be capable of company
With your phantasm, more real then than life;
And be a wild mad woman, if those fears,
Those weary absences, those partings pale,
And fevered expectations, which have filled
The summer of our life with storm and cold,
Determine not in peace and halcyon days.
You do not love me as I love you; no;
Else you would never leave me. Love of power
And love of me hold tourney in your breast.
Let Will throw down the baton, and declare
The love of me the winner, and I'll be
Your queen of love; and beautiful as love
For man can make a woman. I am proud:
When love transfigures me I can conceive
How beautiful I am. Stay with me, then,
That holy, sweet, and confident desire
May light me up a pleasant bower for you:
I am, when you are gone, a house forlorn,
Cold, desolate, and hasting to decay:
Stay, tenant me, preserve me in repair;
Only sweet uses keep sweet beauty fair.

BRUCE

I love you, Isabella, by high heaven,
More than the highest power that can be mine.

ISABELLA
Why then pursue this power so ardently?

BRUCE
I stayed pursuit; but it would follow me.
My countrymen have asked me to be king.

ISABELLA
King!—But you murdered Comyn.
All his friends—
Forgive me, love. I would not for the world
Reproach you; but—

BRUCE
I know your gentle heart.
My thought of you is not the morning bride;
Nor even the rose that oped its balmy breast
And gave its nectar sweetly. In my mind
This memory of you crowds out the rest:
The woman who with tender arms embraced
The bloody murderer. I know your heart.

ISABELLA
Hush!

BRUCE
Friends are few; but if my title's good?
Hopeless the cause; but if the cause be just?
I'm glad my hand that did my passion's hest
Has made my mind up for me.

ISABELLA
You'll be king?

BRUCE
Will I be hunted like a common knave
Who stabs his comrade in a drunken brawl
For some rude jest or ruder courtesan,
And, being an outlaw, dies by any hand?
I'd rather be the king; and though I die
The meanest death, be held in memory
As one who, having entered on a course
Of righteous warfare by a gate of shame,
Pursued it with his might, and made amends
For starting false—so far as lay in him;

For out of him his sin is, 'stablished, past,
And by a life's atonement unredeemed.
I do not brood on this. Before you came
I had better thoughts.

ISABELLA
O, I am sad at that!

BRUCE
I love you: not from you those worse thoughts sprang.

ISABELLA
Perhaps they did: for I have sometimes found,
When I have spent an hour in decking me,
But thinking more to please you in my life
Than in my dress, that, coming then to you,
Brimming with tenderness, some thoughtless word,
Or even a look from you, has changed my mood,
And made me deem the world a wilderness;
While this cross glance, or inauspicious tone,
Was but a feint of yours, whose strength of love
Withheld itself, afraid it should undo
Its purpose by endeavouring too much:
And we have parted, discontented both.
But we'll not part now. Say, we shall not part.

BRUCE
Not now. We will be crowned together, queen.

ISABELLA
'But then' succeeds 'not now'; I hope, far off.

BRUCE
We must prepare to go.

ISABELLA
So soon!

BRUCE
Our friends
Await us, chafing doubtless at delay.

ISABELLA
Then I will make a proverb lie for once,
And be on horseback sooner than my lord.

[They go out.

Enter **BRUCE**, **ISABELLA**, and a **SQUIRE**.

BRUCE
Look to our horses while we rest.

[**SQUIRE** goes out.

ISABELLA
How far
Are we before our friends?

BRUCE
See, they appear.

ISABELLA
That little puff of dust?

BRUCE
Our company,
Three miles away I think. The road is straight,
And slopes to us. I hear a hoof—this side.

ISABELLA
It is a solitary knight, but one
Who need not fear to ride afar, alone,
If I may trust a woman's hasty eye.
He is dismounting; he unhelms, he bows;
He seems to know you, and salute you king!

[Enter **SIR JAMES DOUGLAS**.

BRUCE
Douglas! I thought that Paris would retain
For years to come the service of your youth.

DOUGLAS
You speak as one whom some transcending hap
Has shown the high and secret worth of life;
And such am I, or else discourtesy
Alone had greeted me in what you said.
Not with shrunk purse, drained veins, and heart dried-up;
Will—broken-winded; pith-brains; sinews—straw,
From Paris, which unstiffens many a one,
Come I to Scotland, where is need of strength.

A love of noble things—a kind of faith—
A hope, a wish, a thought above the world,
Has swayed me from the mire; and yet I know
It is a miracle I'm not more soiled.

BRUCE
I spoke unworthily of this reply,
And gladly now unsay my hinted charge,
Which, with less thought than commonplace, I made;
Though I should utter nothing now but thought,
For as you judged I see a soul in life.
And what in Scotland do you think to do?

DOUGLAS
Retrieve my lands, avenge my father's death,
And drive the English from its borders. Here
I offer Scotland's king my lance, and here
I vow to be his lady's loyal knight.
You are amazed. They say, ill news spreads fast:
He whom the tidings then will halcyon
Knows of his weal as soon as he his woe.
Is the news good to you that Bruce is king?

BRUCE
The news is good: best, that he's king of you.
I wonder most at that. I stood in arms
Against your father, and but yesterday
I seemed the friend of England.

DOUGLAS
Yesterday
Was once the date of every lasting change.
While you are faithful to the land that's yours,
I swear to serve you faithfully till death.

BRUCE
Another trusty friend when friends are few—
And such a friend! Welcome, a thousand times!

ISABELLA
A happy handselling of our enterprise!
What is the news from England? Have you heard
If Wallace has been judged?

DOUGLAS
Not yet; but soon
In Westminster he will be doomed to death;
For victory, which oft ennobles kings,

Debases Edward. Since he has not grace,
The gracious-hearted world with one outcry
Should claim the life of Wallace for its own,
As the most noble life lived in this age,
And not to be cut off by one man's hate.

BRUCE
The thought of Wallace troubles me. The truth
That great men seldom in their times are known;
And this that little men are eminent
In midst of their thin lives and loud affairs,
Assert how perilous election is
By peers all bound and circumstanced alike.
If he were solely moved by noble thoughts,
And is the signal hero you give out—
Nothing I say, and nothing I deny—
Then were the nobles who deserted him
Unworthy cowards, beggars, churls, knaves, hounds.
Shall I condemn my order so? or think
That Wallace hoped to aggrandise himself,
And lost those friends who had no need to fight
For mere existence when the restive hoof
Of personal ambition kicked aside
The patriot's caparison? You wince:
But with the time I drift, and cannot find
A mooring for my judgment. Pardon me.
This I believe: there is no warrior
Before the world, who could, even with those means
Of formal power that Wallace mostly lacked,
Have wrought the tithe of his accomplishment:
His name will be an ensign; and his acts
The inspiration of his countrymen.

DOUGLAS
You yet will know his magnanimity
Which girdled round the ample continent
Of his performance like the boundless sea.

BRUCE
I'm glad to think—to know the best of him.
Shall we turn back and meet our friends?

ISABELLA
Yes; come.
And, Douglas, tell us more of Wallace, pray.

[They go out.

Enter the **EARL** and the **COUNTESS OF BUCHAN**, and the **EARL OF FIFE**.

COUNTESS OF BUCHAN
Once more, I beg you, brother, on my knees, To
undertake the duty of your race.
Now, while I plead, they may be crowning him,
And no Macduff to gird his curling hair.
Eleven kings from Malcolm Canmore's time
Our ancestors have perfected with gold,
Laying the ruddy chaplet on their brows
Like magic dawn that tops the day with light.
It is a custom that has come to mean
The thing it garnished; and he cannot be
The King of Scots, however just his claim,
However consecrated, sceptred, throned,
Who is not crowned by you.

FIFE
I am the friend
Of England, of your husband; finally
Be answered I beseech you. If you plead
Again with such hot vehemence, I'll think
Your husband is a fool to slight the word
That birds have carried of the Bruce and you.

COUNTESS OF BUCHAN
If I were richer than to need your help,
I'd let you know that brother's quality
Who dares to doubt his mother's daughter. Shame!
But I am passionate, and so are you:
You meant no wrong. You'll do this, will you not?

FIFE
Why! here's a woman!—What a woman! Well!
I tell you I am England's friend, which means
The foe of any upstart such as Bruce;
And I am Buchan's friend, which means the foe
Of Buchan's mortal foe, the outlaw Bruce.
I tell you this, and yet you beg of me
To do for Bruce the service needed most
To make him mighty in his enmity.

COUNTESS OF BUCHAN
If you were armed to fight a champion,

And he had lost his helm before you met,
You would not do despite to chivalry,
And take advantage of his naked head,
But find him in a morion, or unclasp
Your own, and equally defended, charge.
Be chivalrous to Bruce; make him a king
That Edward may be vantageless in that.
Then fight for Edward—with your puissance, fight.

FIFE
I think you're mad. This pertinacity,
Which you intend shall urge me to comply—
Which you conceive no doubt a sign of strength,
But which I judge a sign of vanity—
Is one of women's weapons, well-approved,
With which she jags to death a stronger will.
But my resolve is harnessed, and your dart
Turns off it blunt—and spent I hope.

BUCHAN
You hear;
I said you could not move him.—Come away—
I'm sorry you have set your mind on this.

[**FIFE** and **BUCHAN** go out.

COUNTESS OF BUCHAN
To toss my hair, to weep, to rate my maid,
Are small reliefs I ne'er resorted to;
And now I must do something notable.
What if I went and crowned the Bruce myself?
Ah! here's a thought that's like a draught of wine!
My brother whose the office is, resiles:
Mine—mine it is!—But how?—but if I did?
Their tongues, their tongues! their foul imaginings!
Is the world wicked as its thought is? Love?
There's no one would believe me if I vowed
Upon my deathbed, between heaven and earth,
I understand no meaning in the word.
Maidens have lovers, and they sigh and wake;
Wives love their husbands, and they wake and weep:
But never, never have I loved a man
As I see women love—with bursting hearts,
With fire and snow at variance in their cheeks,
With arching smiles, the heraldry of joy,
Whose rainbow shadows shine on hot, hard tears;
With cruel passion, dying ecstasy,
With rapture of the resurrection morn.

I have not loved. It may be to my shame,
But justly to the world's, condemning me
For deeds no cause could work me to commit.
If I take horse to Scone, farewell my fame,
Which halts yet at the threshold. Who's this?

[Enter **JAMES CROMBE**.

Crombe,
Do you remember in my father's house
Your life once stood in danger for a crime—
Which I'll not name—when mercy at my plea
Was meted you in place of punishment?

CROMBE
Well I remember.

COUNTESS OF BUCHAN
You were thankful then,
And held your life at my command. The time——

CROMBE
My lady, if some service you require
Perilling my life, I'll do it willingly;
But had you urged my love, my duteous love,
And not my debt, I had been happier.

COUNTESS OF BUCHAN
I beg your pardon, sir. Indeed, I think
The service I require may cost your life,
But surely something dearer. I am whirled
From thought to thought: my mind lacks breath. Good Crombe,
You owe me nothing. Will you, if I bid,
Procure me black dishonour, and yourself
A name of loathing?

CROMBE
No, my lady.

COUNTESS OF BUCHAN
How?

CROMBE
If I beheld you hurrying to your shame,
I'd keep your honour holy with my sword,
And send it hot to heaven.

COUNTESS OF BUCHAN

Well.—You're a Scot?
I mean, you long for Scotland's freedom.

CROMBE
Yes.

COUNTESS OF BUCHAN
Are you acquainted with the news?

CROMBE
Of Bruce?
I've heard they mean to crown him king to-day;
But since my lord of Fife is England's friend——

COUNTESS OF BUCHAN
Yes, yes! But are you glad?

CROMBE
Most heartily.
I think of joining Bruce.

COUNTESS OF BUCHAN
My timorous heart,
Fie, fie!—I knew you were a noble man.
You will put no construction but the right
On what I mean to do. Both you and I
Must be dishonoured in the world's regard:
I, an unfaithful wife; you, go-between.
Saddle two horses; lead them secretly
A mile beyond the castle. There I'll mount
And ride with you to Scone. Go, instantly.
I, Isobel Macduff, will crown Bruce king.

CROMBE
But, noble lady—not for fear, but safety—
What of pursuit?

COUNTESS OF BUCHAN
Pursuit? I am a mint,
And coin ideas. Come—come out! It's gold!
My husband's horses must be aired to-day.
You'll see it done. Some of the grooms we'll bribe,
And some will come unbought, and some we'll force
Either to follow us, or quit their steeds:
Leave nothing in the stables that can run.
My lords—ha! ha!—are nowhere in the chase.

CROMBE

Captain, and countess, mistress, service-worthy,
Be confident in me, as I in you,
And the deed's done.

[Goes out.

COUNTESS OF BUCHAN
Now, world, wag, wag your tongues!
I sacrifice my fame to make a king:
And he will raise this nation's head again
That lies so low; and they will honour him;
And afterwards, perhaps, they'll honour me.
Or if they slight me and my modest work,
I shall be dead: I have enough to bear
Of disrespect and slander here to-day,
Without forecasting railing epitaphs.
But some—nay, many of the worthiest,
And many simple judgments too, will see
The sunlight on my deed. This, I make sure:
No Scot's allegiance can be held from Bruce
Because he was not crowned by a Macduff.—
And if I love him, what is that to him?
That's a good saying. So is this, I make:
If I do love him, what is that to me!

[Goes out.

ACT III

SCENE I.—Westminster. The Hall of the Palace

KING **EDWARD I** on a throne of state. In attendance, **LORDS PEMBROKE**, **PERCY**, **CLIFFORD**, and other **LORDS**, **GENTLEMEN**, and **OFFICERS**.

Enter **SIR PETER MALLORIE** with **SIR WILLAIM WALLACE**, bound and guarded.

EDWARD I
Proceed with the impeachment, Mallorie.

MALLORIE
Sir William Wallace, knight of Elderslie,
Some time usurping Guardian of Scotland,
You are a traitor to the English crown—

WALLACE
I am no traitor to the English crown,

For I was never subject to King Edward.

MALLORIE
Therein your treason rests. But speak not now:
You may speak afterwards in your defence.

WALLACE
I will speak now, not to excuse my deeds,
But to arraign the falsest traitor here.
Edward of England, if one pure pulse beats
In that debauched and enervated core
Which was your conscience, I will make it ache.

EDWARD I
What do you mean? To have us think you mad,
And to your frailty that compassion show
Which crimes and sins forbid us to extend?
Or are you posing as a prodigy
Of heroism? In their minstrelsy
They sing of captive knights whose bold address
In presence of their victors won them grace:
But know that justice sees no worth in words—
Deeds only: therefore hear your deeds rehearsed.

MALLORIE
Sir William Wallace, treasons manifold—

WALLACE
I crave the pardon of all manhood here.
Having small use for any faculty
Since I became a captive, I have slacked
The rigour of my will, and thus it is
I spoke with petulance before my time.
Proceed to read my accusation, sir.

MALLORIE
You are accused of many treasonous acts
Done on the persons, castles, cities, lands,
Of our most noble sovereign, Edward First,
In England and in Scotland—

WALLACE
But, explain—

EDWARD I
Silence, guilty felon!

WALLACE

Guilty? Condemned
And hanged already, doubtless, in your heart.
I will confess my guilt, for I am guilty—
Guilty of failure in a righteous cause.
I will confess that when ill-fortune came
My friends forsook me; that I lost the day
At Falkirk, and have since been little worth.
I stayed your accusation, sir, to ask
What treason I could work against a king
Whom I acknowledge not, and in a land
Not governed by that king?

EDWARD I
Silence!—Proceed.

WALLACE
What! English Edward! Would you roar me down?
My deeds have spoken: shall I fear your tongue?
The charge against me is irrelevant;
No jurisdiction have you over me
To pardon or to doom: prisoner of war,
No traitor, I; and here I make demand
For knightly treatment at the hands of knights.

EDWARD I
You shall have justice.

WALLACE
In the end I shall:
And so shall you. Death you have often faced;
Justice you shall see once.

EDWARD I
Stay, Mallorie.
We'll tutor this heroic insolence.
The observant world has notched the life of man,
And three main periods indicate three powers
Whose dreadful might directs our very stars.
These powers take reason's throne, the intellect.
First, love usurps, like Saturn come again—
Whose orb is yet man's most malignant foe—
Turning the sad, outlandish time of youth
Into a golden age. Ambition rules
With godly sway the second period,
And marshals man's capacity to war
Against the evils that beset him most,
And win what things of worship he desires.
Prudence, which none but old men understand

To be the strongest tyrant of the three,
Reigns lastly, making peace with God and man:
Securing acquisitions; peering forth
Into the future, like a mariner,
Whose freight is landed in a foreign port,
With wistful homeward gaze, but eager yet
To see his merchandise disposed of well:
And reason, which should rule, most cheerfully
Accepts the ministry beneath these kings:
That is the chronicle of noble men.
The sun gleams lurid through a rotting fog,
And those pure powers that shine in lucent souls,
Clear, as if lanterned only by the air,
In natures base, burn with a murky flame,
As lust, concupiscence, and avarice:
And reason, mad with degradation, toils
Unwillingly in slavish offices.
Now comes my application. Cruel, vain,
Intolerant, unjust, false, murderous,
You, Wallace—rebel, outlaw, hangman, fool,
Incendiary, reiver, ravisher—
You are the serf of vile concupiscence—
Yea, of the vilest famine—hungry greed
Of notoriety!—the commonest,
The meanest, lewdest, gauntest appetite,
That drives the ignoble to extremity!
No sooner had we quarried painfully
Forth of that chaos left by your King John,
A corner-stone for righteous government,
Than you and other itching malcontents
With gothic hands o'erturned the fane of peace
And on your groaning land brought heathen war,
That you might win the name of patriot.
Again I built up order; and again
You overthrew my government, and caused
Your fatherland—heroic patriot!—
From Tweed to Moray Firth to swim in blood,
Before divine authority could rule.
Still you rebelled; for you must stand alone—
And think not, lords, I over-rate the strength
Of this delirious thirst for some repute—
Though nobles, knights, burgesses, yeomen, priests,
Yea, every Scot, well-pleased, acknowledged us,
You—cast-off guardian—dog that had his day—
Alone, unfriended, starving in the wilds,
Held there aloof, and signalised your night
By howling for that moon you almost clutched,
A tyrant's power, calling it liberty:

For that was still behind your lust of fame.

MALLORIE
You're silent now.

A LORD
Silence becomes him well.
This just exposure stills his shameful voice.

WALLACE
Seeing how your rage leapt from your lips in lies,
King, I bethink me ere I make reply,
Lest I, too, throw the truth.

EDWARD I
Now tell us, lords,
Are we on our defence or Wallace? Which?
Villain, regard law's form if not its soul.
Be better mannered; touch your memory;
You stand before the majesty of England.

WALLACE
I stand there truly; but behind me pants
The king of terrors; and his quiver holds
One dart I hope to parry, which I fear—
But not the venomed shaft that nothing fends.
It is—not now; I'll tell you afterwards.—
Noble?—ignoble?—who shall judge us, king?
This deed and that we may with help of heaven
Christen or damn, and not be far astray;
But who shall take upon him to declare
The mind of God on what is unrevealed,
The guiding thought, deep, secret, which is known,
Even to the thinker, but in passing wafts.
Because my life was spent in thwarting you,
I am not therefore an incarnate fiend,
Although the justice of the end I stayed
Possessed your soul to sickening. Mad for fame!—
My wife's, my father's, and my brother's deaths.—

EDWARD I
No more of this. Call in the witnesses.

WALLACE
I'll speak now, and be heard.

ALL
Silence! Be still.

WALLACE

I can outroar you all. Sound trumpets, drums,
And fill your hall with clamour, I shall speak,
And you shall hear. Above the voice of war
I have been heard, and—

ALL

Silence, traitor, silence!

[The shouting continues for a little, but gradually ceases as **WALLACE** speaks on.

WALLACE

I fought for liberty and not for fame.
Monarchs know not the inestimable worth
Of that imperial, rich diadem
Which only crowns both kings and carls, men.
Say, slavery unfelt were possible,
Then freedom is a name for sounding wind.
But call me slave in any mincing term;
And let the tyrant's frowns be smiles of love;
The chains, less galling than a lady's arms;
The labour, just my pleasure's ministry:
If I surrender to the conqueror,
As captive is my soul, as though thick irons
Wore through my flesh, and rusting in my blood,
Rasped on my bones, the while with lash and oath
Some vicious tasker held me to hard toil.
I stand here free, though bound and doomed to die.
And know, King Edward, every Scot who bent,
Gnawing his heart, a recreant knee to you,
Perjured himself, being free; and even now—
I know my countrymen—contrite they rise;
And when they have another leader—one
Abler than I—pray heaven, more fortunate!—
They will anew throw off your galling yoke,
And be once more lieges of liberty.
I am the heart of Scotland; when I die
It shall take heart again—

EDWARD I

No, no! by heaven!
The Scots repudiate you!

WALLACE

The Scots do not:
The people, pulse for pulse, beat warm with me.

EDWARD I

You lie! You lie!—But I forgot myself.
Freebooters, prodigals, scroyles—outcasts all—
Your sole supporters, may lament your end;
But true men everywhere are jubilant.
Not England only, and the better part
Of your divided country were your foes;
But from the world's beginning you were doomed
To fail in your unholy enterprise.
For destiny, whose servant Nature is,
Ordained by the creation of this land—
So long sore vexed by chance, fate's enemy,
With heptarchies, divisions, kings and clans—
That one king and one people here should dwell,
Clasped in the sea's embrace, happy and safe
As heaven is, anchored in eternity.
In fighting me you fought fate's champion,
Anointed with the fitness of the time,
And with the strength of his desire inspired,
To finish Nature's work in Albion.
You, paltry minion of a band of knaves,
In name of patriotism—which in this case
Was in the devil's name—fought against God;
The coming of His kingdom hindered here.
Now His sure vengeance has o'ertaken you,
And over both our lands His sweet peace reigns.

WALLACE

Eternal God, record this blasphemy!
Who doubts our lands are destined to be one?
Who does not pray for that accomplishment!
Why! Know you not that is the period,
The ultimate effect I battled for,
That you, free English, and that we, free Scots,
May one day be free Britons. And we shall;
For Scotland never will be tributary:
We are your equals, not to be enslaved;
We are your kin, your brothers, to be loved.
Time is not ripe: fate's crescent purposes,
Like aloe-trees, bloom not by forcing them;
But seasonable changes, mellowing years,
Elaborative ages, must mature
The destined blossoms. Listen, king and lords;
Here is a thing worthy remembering,
And which perhaps you never rightly knew:
Duty is always to the owner done;
And the immediate debtor wisely pays:
The heritage of duty unperformed

Increases out of sight of usury.
Restore to Scotland freedom. Do that, king,
Or it will be required from you or yours
With woeful interest.—I have done. I feared
I might not find a way to speak these truths,
Having no nimble tongue, and die oppressed
With warning unpronounced. I truly thought
I could command a hearing had I words.
Death now, the due of all, my triumph, waits.

EDWARD I
The witnesses, Sir Peter Mallorie;
Your accusation now is needless.

MALLORIE
Sire,
Hugh Beaumont is the first. He'll testify
Of early deeds in the arch-traitor's life.
He is an old man now and garrulous:
A gentleman withal, whose gentle blood
Stood him in little stead, when windy youth
Had sown itself, and whirling poverty
Down to the barren common dashed his head.
So with his sword he battened as he might,
And valour was his star. Let him have scope,
For he has much to say.

[**HUGH BEAUMONT** is led in.

Inform the king
As strictly as to God of all that passed
Between you and the prisoner.

EDWARD I
Speak the truth.

BEAUMONT
Your gracious majesty, what I can tell
Is liker fable; but the noble knight,
The prisoner, will acknowledge all I say:
Much of it honours him.—To Ayr he came
One day, disguised, with hat down, cloak pulled up.
There as he paced the street, Lord Percy's man
Seized on some fish a burgher just had bought;
Whereat, Sir William, like a smouldering fire,
Flared up to burn the foot whose thoughtless kick
Had tortured it to flame. In speechless rage
He grasped the caitiff's throat and smote him dead.

About two score well-harnessed Englishmen,
With whom I was, did straight environ him.
Against a wall he bore which seemed to be
Rather upheld by him than him upholding,
And reaped us down like corn. He did, my lords.
He multiplied his strokes so that he seemed
To multiply himself; there did appear
Opposed to every soldier there a Wallace.
Without or helm or mail, in summer-weed,
Grass-green, flowered red with blood, he fought us all,
Till one that bit the dust writhed near enough
To pierce him in the leg, and then he fell.
Yet even so he might have won away;
But as he rose he fetched a blow at me,
Which I eluding, down his breaking brand
Upon the causeway struck; and in his eyes
A light went out, when his uplifted hand
Showed but the hilt. In faith I pitied him,
I pitied him, and bore him to the tower.
There in a filthy dungeon he expired
Of festering wounds and food that swine refused,
Ere they had settled what death was his due.

EDWARD I
But he is here alive?

BEAUMONT
Pardon, dread lord;
He seemed at that time dead: the West mourned for him:
His aged nurse bought his corrupting corpse
To bury it decently in hallowed ground.
Well, after that a while, in Lanark town,
I waited in the High Street on the judge,
Lord Ormesby, then on circuit in the West.
Four men were with me. One, on fire with wine,
A braggart at the best, vaunted his deeds.
And when two men came down the street, he cried,
"See yonder stalks a canny muffled Scot,
A strapper, by this light! attended, too!
He's like to have that may be taxable.
Something I'll mulct him of; or something give,
That shall be worse than nothing—namely, blows!"
"Belike," said I, "that boon will not go quit.
His side is guarded by a lengthy purse,
Whose bright contents, I think, he will not hoard."
"I'll have his sword," quoth he, "if he refuse,
Take it, and beat him with it till he shake
His dastard body out of his habergeon;

Which, leaving here, he'll give me hearty thanks,
That I leave him his skin, the lousy Scot!"
And so he staggered out to meet the two.
The muffled stranger whispered to his man,
And he sped on before in anxious haste,
Dodging the drunk man's outstretched arm, who said,
"Well, you may go; your master is behind."
And when the master came he stopped him, saying,
"Knave Scot, unveil! Come, show your sonsy face.
Vile thief, where did you steal this tabard green?
And where the devil got you this fair knife?
What! jewelled in the hilt! Unbuckle, quick,
Mantle and whittle; and to make amends
For having ever worn them, clasp them both
About me, and you shall have leave to go."
"St. Andrew! There's my whittle, English dog!"
And with a thrust the Scot let out his life.
We others rushed upon him instantly,
Shouting, "Down with him! Vengeance on the
Scot!" He gave us back, "St. Andrew, and the right!"
Wrapping his arm in what had wrapped his face,
And looking like the lion that he was.
Beholding him, I trembled, and stood still;
But one more rash ran on, to shriek and fall,
His raised right arm lopped at the shoulder off.
With that a voice cried, "In the king's name, peace!"
The Scot looked up and saw a troop approach.
"Too great a pack for one," he said, and ran.
Now this was Ormesby, the justiciary,
Arrived in Lanark to dispense the law,
With Hazelrig, the ruler of the shire.

MALLORIE [Aside to **BEAUMONT**]
Quick, man! be quick! Look how his Highness chafes!

BEAUMONT
The valiant Scot was Wallace.
It appeared
His foster-mother, who had paid away
The earnings of her lifetime for his corpse,
Kissing and weeping o'er it, saw a spark
Struggle with night of death; or else her hope
Inspired new breath, much aided by her prayers.
The little glow she nursed into a flame,
So feeble, that, lest meat should smother it,
Her daughter gave one of her bosom's springs,
Then at high-tide to feed her new-born babe,
For the replenishing his body's lamp.

Being recovered, he had come to see
His wife, who dwelt in Lanark.

WALLACE [Aside]
God! O God!

BEAUMONT
Hazelrig led the chase: I followed close.
We reached the house: I searched the garden. There,
Scarcely concealed, I saw the prisoner.
Sire, I'm not a coward, and I was not then;
But from the instant that I recognised
The dead man come alive, enchantment caught
My spirit in a toil, and made me watch,
Powerless and voiceless, all he did. I felt
No movement, even while I followed him.
There was some witchery I do believe.
In by the window, when the search was o'er,
He entered, saying gaily to his wife,
"I almost think an English lourdane saw me.
How thin a thicket hides a dread discovery!"
Then seeing on the floor his lady lie,
"O God! what varied truth was in that word!
Not dead, my love!" She spoke that I could hear.
"Dying, dying. Hazelrig has killed me.
My spirit clings still to my lips to kiss you.
I would my soul might melt into a kiss
To lie on your lips till your soul's release,
And then to heaven together we would fly.
Avenge my death and Scotland's wrongs." "My love!"
He cried; and all his strength was water.
And long he held her: and he shook and sobbed.

WALLACE [Straining his bonds]
Nay, hang me!—burn me!—I am sawn asunder!

BEAUMONT
At length he put her softly on a seat,
And took her hand and knelt: and she was dead:
Her face was like an angel's fallen asleep.
Upon her bloody breast his eyes he fixed,
Seeming unruffled as a still white flame,
And words, more dread than silence, spake aloud:
"I will avenge thy death and Scotland's wrongs.
For every tear that now my eyes have dropped
From English veins shall seas of blood be shed.
Each sigh of mine shall have ten thousand echoes:
Yea, for her death I'll England sepulchre.

O glutton grave, a surfeit shall be thine!
Death's self shall sleep before my vengeance flags."
Slowly retiring, with his face to her,
He went. I have not seen him since till now.
He was a young man then.

[**VOICES** within.

EDWARD I
What noise is that?

CLIFFORD
A messenger, my lord, would force the door.

EDWARD I
Whence comes he?

CLIFFORD
From the North, your majesty.

EDWARD I
Admit him.

[Enter **MESSENGER**.

Welcome, sir. Your news at once,
Plainly and nakedly.

MESSENGER
Comyn is dead:
Slain in Dumfries by Bruce; whose party then,
Led by the fiery Edward, mad as he,
Attacked and seized the castle. On the day
I left the North, in Scone, the Lady Buchan,
The Bruce's paramour, Fife's sister, crowned
Her murderous lover king. Some lords and knights
Have gathered round him, and he lies at Perth.

EDWARD I
Besotted fool! But it is well. Herein
I see God's hand hardening the heart of Bruce
Against me, who am but God's minister,
That I may cut him off. I give God thanks.
Wallace—What! has he swooned?

MALLORIE
He's in a trance.
Wallace!—Well, this is strange!—Wallace!

WALLACE [Starting]
My lords!

EDWARD I
We'll countenance this mockery no more.
All England and all Scotland—all the world
Prejudge your fate. Wherefore we will not then
Waste time in tedious processes of law
To find you, as we know you, dyed in guilt,
And leave another to pursue unchecked
A course of similar iniquity.
You for your treason are condemned to die
The death that traitors merit. Lead him hence.
Come after me, my lords, immediately,
And take your charges for the North.

[**EDWARD I** goes out. **WALLACE** is led away.

CLIFFORD
I think
The king but whiled the time with Wallace here
Till news should come from Scotland.

PEMBROKE
With what haste
He sentenced him!

PERCY
Yes; as a gamesome cat
Diverted with a mouse, scenting another,
Gobbles the captive quick.

[ALL go out.

ACT IV

SCENE I.—A Room in the Earl of Buchan's Castle

Enter the **EARL OF BUCHAN**

BUCHAN
This is not jealousy. I only ache
With sorrow that my trust has been reposed
In falseness; and I feel—I fear I feel
The whole world's finger, quivering with scorn,

Stream venom at me. If I cannot sleep,
It is no wonder, for the laugh I hear,
Like icy water rippling—cold and true
As tested steel—so wise, so absolute—
Is learned from those that know me by the fiend
Who watches with me nightly. Jealousy?
If it possessed me, mortal sickness, bonds,
Nothing in heaven or hell, would hold me back
From sating it with blood—with hers and his.
But I will not be jealous, like poor souls,
Whose vanity engrosses every thought,
And calls itself nobility; not I.
I will devise some vengeance, some just means,
Some condign punishment, the world will praise,
Thinking of me more highly than before
This miserable time.

[Enter **FIFE**.

FIFE
Brooding again!
Pluck up some sprightliness, for I have news.
Pembroke has routed Bruce in Methven wood,
And captured many leading rebels. Bruce,
Who showed himself a gallant warrior,
Proved in retreat wise as a veteran,
Escaping to the North.

BUCHAN
My wife?

FIFE
They say
That she and other ladies northward too
In Nigel Bruce's charge escaped with speed.

BUCHAN
And is this sure?

FIFE
I well believe it. Come,
Question the man who told me.

BUCHAN
If it's true
We'll join our powers and hunt the rebels down
Like noxious vermin, as they are.

FIFE
Be cool.
What means this bitter passion?

BUCHAN
Am I hot?
But you'll combine with me?

FIFE
Assuredly:
It is a noble chase; the quarry, game
To wind us over Scotland. Tally-ho!

BUCHAN
Now you are thoughtless. Come, the messenger.

[They go out.

SCENE II.—The Wood of Drome. Scotch Soldiers About a Watch-Fire

1st SOLDIER
What clouted loons we are! Royal beadsmen! Eh?

2nd SOLDIER
The king's as ragged as the rest.

1st SOLDIER
That's true. to-day I hunted with him, and I thought, Seeing his doublet loop-holed, frayed, and fringed; His swaddled legs and home-made shoes of pelt; His barbarous beard and hair, and freckled face, That manhood's surely more than royalty; For through this weedy, nettle-grown decay, A majesty appeared that distanced us, Even as a ruined palace overbears A hamlet's desolation.

[Enter **BRUCE**, unperceived.

3rd SOLDIER
He's a king
By nature, though descent were lost in churls.

2nd SOLDIER
Ay, ay; but mark: I'll reason of our state.
Here many days we've wasted in the wild,
Chased by the English like the deer we chase,
Exposed like them, without their native wont,
Beneath this fickle, rigorous northern clime,
Ill-fed, ill-clad, and excommunicate;
While decent burghers—Scots as true as we—

Live warm, and prosper with their families.
I think we're fools.

1st SOLDIER
Fools for ourselves, maybe,
But wise I hope for Scotland: and the folk
In every town and village think us wise,
And bless and pray for us.

BRUCE [Aside]
A brave heart that.
[Advancing]
Good evening, comrades. Can you guess the time?

1st SOLDIER
An hour past sunset. Look, your Majesty;
Barred by these trunks the cloudy embers burn
Where day is going out.

BRUCE
Faintly I see.
Your fire's so bright it dims the distant glow.
Sit down again, good friends.

1st SOLDIER
A story, sir?

2nd SOLDIER
O, pray you tell us one!

BRUCE
I think I will.
I've told you many tales of chivalry,
Of faerie, and of Greeks and Romans too;
But now I'll tell you of a Scotchman—one
Who lived when Rome was most puissant here.
The Roman governor, a valiant man,
Agricola, in whom ambition paused
Whenever prudence thought the utmost done,
Reconquered all the southern British tribes,
And drove his enemy beyond the Forth.
The noble Galgacus then swayed the realm
That stretches northward of that winding stream;
And while the Roman, building forts and walls,
As was his wont, secured the bird in hand,
He mustered from his glens a skin-clad host
To fight for freedom. Ardoch they call it,
Where the armies met. Ere the battle joined,

Firm on his chariot-floor with voice aflame,
The Scottish chief harangued his thirty thousand.
"Brothers," he cried, "behold your enemies!
Gauls, Germans, Britons—mercenaries, slaves!
In conquest, one and strong; but in defeat,
So many weaklings, heartless, hopeless, lost.
One signal victory to us were more
Than all the battles that our foes have won:
Their confidence is in their leader; ours,
In our cause. Hearken!—had I a voice,
Like heaven's thunder, I would shout across
This battle-field to be, to yon mixed throng,
And tell them they are Britons, Germans, Gauls:
Bid them remember how in haughty Rome
Their free-born countrymen are taught to serve
The wanton fancies of luxurious vice
In perfumed chambers or in bloody shows;
Think of their wives and daughters, all abused;
Think of themselves, leagued with their conquerors
Armed and opposed against consanguine folk,
Placed in the van to bear the battle's brunt,
That Rome may triumph, and her blood not shed:
Then would they turn and rend with us the foe.
What need has Rome of Britain? we, of Rome?
We, the last lonely people of the North,
A morsel merely, perilous and far,
Incite the eagle appetite of Rome,
Uncloyed until she gorges all the world.
No other need has Rome. Poor, desolate,
Shrouded with mists, with cold empanoplied,
At war among ourselves, fighting with beasts,
We yet are freemen; and we need not Rome:
We are the only freemen in the world.
Here, in the very bosom of our land—
The last land in the world—we meet the power
That rules all other lands but ours. Even here
Let Rome be stricken. Brothers, countrymen,
Freedom has taken refuge in our hills.
She has a home upon the streaming seas,
But loves the land where men are hers. Let not
The word go forth on woeful-sounding winds
That Rome has driven freedom from the earth:
Sprite you with lions' hearts; like baleful stars
Inflame your eyes that their disastrous glance
May palsy foes afar; pour your whole strength
In every blow, nor fear a drought: the power
Of each is great as all when all are one.
Rush like a torrent; crash like rocks that fall

When thunder rends the Grampians. Liberty!
Cry 'Liberty!' and shatter Rome."
The Scots were worthy of their gallant chief,
And fought as if they loved death, courting her
By daring her to opportunities;
Which she—a maid o'er-wooed—resented oft,
And strained their cooler rivals to her breast;
But discipline—that rock that bears the world,
Compactly built—a city on a cliff
Breaking disorder back like unknit waves—
Founded the Roman power; and on its front
The Scots beat, shivered by their own onset;
And evening saw them ebb, calmed, vanquished, spent.
Yet that lost battle was a gain: our hills,
That battle, and the ruin of her fleet,
Held Rome behind Grahame's dyke, and kept us Scots.
All south of us the Romans, Saxons, Danes,
And Normans, conquering in turn, o'erthrew
From change to change; but we are what we were
Before Aeneas came to Italy,
Free Scots; and though this great Plantagenet
Seems now triumphant, we will break his power.
Shall we not, comrades?

1st SOLDIER
Yes, your Majesty.

2nd SOLDIER
But might it not have been a benefit
If Rome had conquered Scotland too, and made
Between the Orkneys and the Channel Isles
One nation?

BRUCE
A subtle question, soldier;
But profitless, requiring fate unwound.
It might be well were all the world at peace,
One commonwealth, or governed by one king;
It might be paradise; but on the earth
You will not find a race so provident
As to be slaves to benefit their heirs.

1st SOLDIER
At least we will not.

BRUCE
By St. Andrew, no!

[Enter **NIGEL BRUCE**.

My brother Nigel! Happy and amazed
I see you here. Why left you Aberdeen?

NIGEL
For several ends. And firstly, I have news.

BRUCE
Come to our cave.

NIGEL
No; for a reason, no.

BRUCE
Mysteries, secrets!—Well; retire good friends.

[**SOLDIERS** go out.

NIGEL
Perhaps my news is stale.

BRUCE
Little I know
Since in the flight from Methven, panic-struck,
We parted company.

NIGEL
Learn then that Haye—
Hugh de la Haye; John is with you, I know—
Inchmartin, Fraser, Berclay, Somerville,
Young Randolf, Wishart, trusty Lamberton
Are captives.

BRUCE
Half my world! But is it true?

NIGEL
So much is certainty. Rumour declares
Young Randolf has deserted us; that those
I named will ransom; but that some, unknown,
Have died the death of traitors.

BRUCE
Noble souls!
Randolf—poor boy! What more?

NIGEL

A price
Is on your head.

BRUCE
That matters not.

NIGEL
I know.
Still, have great heed of whom and how you trust.
That's all the evil tidings. Hear the good.
The queen—Ah, this is she! I'll leave you now.

[Goes out.

[Enter **ISABELLA**.

BRUCE
My dearest!

ISABELLA
I couldn't wait, my husband.
The Lady Douglas and the Lady Buchan
Are in your cave. We rode from Aberdeen
This evening, learning you were cantoned here.
Douglas was sleeping when we came. His wife
Bent o'er him, and she slipped into his dream;
For when he waked he wondered not at all
To see his lady there, till memory
Aroused him quite to find the vision true.
Nigel was seeking you; but when I saw
The joy these two partook, incontinent
I hurried out myself to find like cheer.
My dear wayfaring hero, I have come
To share your crust, and rags, and greenwood couch:
I'm deep in love with skied pavilions:
I'll be your shepherdess, Arcadian king.
This evening's journey lay throughout a wood:
The honeysuckle incensed all the air,
And cushats cooed in every fragrant fir;
Tall foxgloves nodded round the portly trees,
Like ruffling pages in the trains of knights;
Above the wood sometimes a green hill peered,
As if dame Nature on her pillow turned
And showed a naked shoulder; all the way,
Whispering along, rose-bushes blushed like girls
That pass blood-stirring secrets fearfully,
Attending on a princess in her walk;
I think with rarely scented breath they said

A loving wife was speeding to her lord.
Why are you silent?

BRUCE
I am thinking, dear,
That I'm the richest monarch in the world.
Possessing such a universe of love,
The treasure most desired by kings and clowns.

ISABELLA
What universe, dear lord?

BRUCE
Simplicity!
You are my universe of love, you know.

ISABELLA
Then keep your universe, and do not waste
In empty space the time. I'll stay with you;
Surely I can? Come, tell me all your plans.

BRUCE
I've none. What I desire I know; and think
Firmly and honestly my wish is right.
Plans are for gods and rich men: I am poor.

ISABELLA
In spirit? So you may be blamelessly;
But are you, sir?

BRUCE
I hardly know. Just now
I tried to cheer a whining fellow here,
But stood myself in greater need of hope.

ISABELLA
I know—I understand. You need to think
Of other things, my dear. I've heard of men,
Great men, exhausted even to lunacy
By just those labours that were beating smooth
A thoroughfare for ever to success,
Repair themselves with youth's prerogative
That stops time and the world deposes, all
In favour of a dream; or spend a while
With children or the simplest souls they knew.
Come, you must be amused. But, tell me, sir,
Am I to stay?

BRUCE
Yes, dearest pilgrim, yes.

ISABELLA
Oh, I am happy! We will live like birds.

BRUCE
And in the winter?

ISABELLA
Winter? What is it?
This is the summer.

BRUCE
Winter is—

ISABELLA
Hush!—hark!
What birds so late fly screaming overhead?

BRUCE
Stout capercailzies, hurrying to their hills,
Sated with fir-tops.

ISABELLA
Ah! But, dearest lord,
Are you quite well? I haven't asked you yet.

BRUCE
I am very well. And you?

ISABELLA
See—look at me:
You used to know by gazing in my eyes.

BRUCE
My wife, my lover, you are well indeed.

ISABELLA
The fire is nearly out. Come to the cave,
And there we will devise amusements, dear.

[They go out.

SCENE III.—Another Part of the Wood of Drome

The **EARL OF BUCHAN** alone.

BUCHAN
God help me and all jealous fools, I pray!
The plagues of Hades leagued in one raw scourge
Might minister diversion to my soul,
Assailing through my flesh. No thought at all
Of starry space or void eternity;
Nor love, nor hate, nor vengeance, nor remorse—
My cousin's murder!—I've forgotten it!—
No sound of horns crackling with riotous breath
The crisp, rathe air; no hounds; no beckoning tunes
With notes of fiery down; nor singing girls
Whose voices brood and bound; nor chanting larks,
Nor hymning nightingales can touch my soul.
Nothing but torture unendurable
Wrought in the flesh has power on jealousy.
Slay him with agonies? A passing swoon!
I'll kill my wife!
Her blood is Lethe if oblivion be
Save in more high-strung anguish of my own.

[Enter **FIFE**.

FIFE
What is it? You have news.

BUCHAN
They are together—
The outlaw and your sister. They're at hand—
Three miles away—no more. A trusty spy
Told me just now.

FIFE
Is there a band?

BUCHAN
Some score.

FIFE
Then we will take them.

BUCHAN
Yes.

FIFE
About it straight.

[Goes.

BUCHAN
I'll follow—Ho!

[Enter **SPY**.

I thought you still were near.
I haven't thanked you yet.

[Gives money.

How did she look?
Was there about her not a thievish air,
A truant aspect, frightened and yet free,
Shame-faced, but bold, and like an angel lost.

SPY
Who, my good lord?

[Re-enter **FIFE**.

BUCHAN
The queen—the outlaw's wife.

SPY
O no, my lord! She laughed, as she rode past
Where I lay hid, at something gaily said
By my good lady, your good lordship's wife.
They both looked happy, riding in the sun.

BUCHAN
Aye; that will do.

[Exit **SPY**.

I'm coming, Fife.

FIFE
Stay yet.
Why did you try to lead him off the scent?
You meant my sister when you questioned him.
Tell me, what makes your jealousy so strong?
You never were in love with her I think.

BUCHAN
Nor am not now. I think—I know—I feel
What I have heard: true love is never jealous.

I am like other men; I love myself.
I cannot speak. I mean to act. Come on.

[They go out.

SCENE IV.—A Cave in the Wood of Drome, with a Fire at the Back

BRUCE, EDWARD, NIGEL BRUCE, DOUGLAS, CROMBE, ISABELLA, COUNTESS OF BUCHAN, LADY DOUGLAS, and others.

BRUCE
Who would build palaces when homes like these
Our kingdom yields us bosomed in her hills!
What tapestry, where the gloss and colour fade
From some love-story, overtold and stale,
Or where a famed old battle stagnates dim,
Befits a room before these unhewn walls
Whose shifting pictures lower and shine and live,
Ruddy and dark in leaping of the fire.
No homely mice in cupboards cheep; the night
Is here not soothed by any mellow chirp
Of crickets, happily, devoutly busy;
But in the ivy and the hollow oak
The owl has heard and learnt through day-long dreams
The wind's high note when pines in ranks are blown,
Bent, rent, and scattered with their roots in air,
And sounds his echo loud and dwindling long,
Fearfully as he flutters past our door;
The wild-cat screams far off in the pheasant's nest;
The wehrwolf, ravening in the warren, growls.
Night is no gossip here, watching the world
Sick-tired, heart-sore, sleep weariness away;
But free and noble, full of fantasy,
Queen of the earth, earth-bound, ethereal.

ISABELLA [Aside]
His spirit rises. We must hold it up.—
My lord, shall Lady Douglas sing?

BRUCE
She shall.
Lady, I beg you sing us something sweet.
No trumpet notes, no war—

[**1st SOLDIER** appears at the entrance of the Cave. **DOUGLAS** whispers with him.

What does he want?

DOUGLAS
He comes as spokesman for his fellows.

BRUCE
Well?

1st SOLDIER [Advancing]
I hope your Highness will be patient with me.
My mates have bade me ask a favour, strange
And difficult to ask; but not so strange
If it be thought of well, nor difficult
If I can keep my head.

BRUCE
Go on.

1st SOLDIER
My lord,
For this great while we have seen no woman's face,
My mates and I: your Highness knows that well.
When we beheld these ladies enter here,
A longing seized us all to look on them;
To see their faces and their gentle shapes;
And even to have them turn their eyes on us;
Perhaps to hear them speak. We are true men,
And honest in our thought.

BRUCE
Bring them all in.

[Exit **1st SOLDIER**.

COUNTESS OF BUCHAN
I know the mood that holds these men: brave lads!
If they were wed to women worth their love,
They would be nobler heroes than they are.

ISABELLA
We'll speak to them.

COUNTESS OF BUCHAN
I'll kiss that knave who spoke.

LADY DOUGLAS
Will you?

COUNTESS OF BUCHAN
Yes; and I'll do it openly.

[Enter **SOLDIERS**.

BRUCE
Welcome all, heartily, most heartily.

COUNTESS OF BUCHAN [To **1st SOLDIER**]
Have you a wife?

1st SOLDIER
I have.

COUNTESS OF BUCHAN
You love her?

1st SOLDIER
Yes.

COUNTESS OF BUCHAN
Is not the truest love the most capricious?

1st SOLDIER
I cannot tell. True love is fanciful.

COUNTESS OF BUCHAN
You long to kiss your wife?

1st SOLDIER
And if I do,
What matters to your ladyship?

COUNTESS OF BUCHAN [Whispering]
This, sir:
I also long to kiss one whom I love;
Perhaps I never shall; but I think now
In kissing you that I am kissing him.

[Kisses him.

1st SOLDIER
Thanks, noble lady. If you were my wife
I'd kiss you thus.

[He embraces and kisses her.

BRUCE

Well said and bravely done!

COUNTESS OF BUCHAN
And can you fight
As deftly as you kiss?

BRUCE
I warrant him!
Your song, my Lady Douglas; sing it now;
A love-song, something homely if you can.

DOUGLAS
Sing "If she love me," sweetheart.

LADY DOUGLAS
Shall I? Well.
But you should sing it rather.

DOUGLAS
No; sing you.

SONG.
Love, though tempests be unruly,
Blooms as when the weather's fair:
If she love me truly, truly,
She will love me in despair.
Is there aught endures here longer?
Can true love end ever wrongly?
Death will make her love grow stronger,
If she love me strongly, strongly.
Can scorn conquer love? Can shame?
Though the meanest tower above me,
She will share my evil fame,
If she love me, if she love me.

[Enter a **FORESTER**.

FORESTER
A thousand men are on you, fly!

[Going.

BRUCE
Stand, there!
Hold him! What thousand men? who lead them? speak.—
Put out the fire—stamp on it, some of you.

[The fire is trampled out and the **FORESTER** seized.

FORESTER
I know not; but I saw them in the wood
Stealthily marching.

BRUCE
Are they near?

FORESTER
An hour
By time, for they are stumbling out a way.
There's half a mile or so of wood between.
If I had been their guide they had been here.

BRUCE
You know the paths so thoroughly?

FORESTER
Blindfold.

BRUCE
Could you lead safely to Kildrummie Castle
A band of twenty?

FORESTER
When? to-night?

BRUCE
Just now.

FORESTER
I think I could. But tell me, sir: they say
That you're the king. Now are you?

BRUCE
I am he.
FORESTER [Awkwardly]
What must I do?

BRUCE
Wait patiently.—Good friends,
We'll yet postpone farewell. A little way
Together in the wood—

EDWARD BRUCE
But must we fly?
Ten are a thousand in a coward's sight;
And they may be our friends. Defence even here

Were not too rash against a hundred. What!
Is not despair achievement's mother? Why!
The high, black night, a shout, a sudden charge,
And we dispel this sheep-heart's fearful dream.

BRUCE
Upon us march the Earls of Fife and Buchan,
With many hundred men. They have hunted us
For days, and I have known. My spies are caught
I fear, or they had not arrived so close
Without our knowledge.
[To **FORESTER**]
We must thank you, friend,
For timely information of our plight.
The plan I formed still holds, and this is it.
Kildrummie will give shelter to our wives;
Nigel will take them there: Douglas, one way,
And I, another, as we may decide,
Splits up the scent,—and we shall all escape.

EDWARD BRUCE
Brother and king—

BRUCE
No more. In straits like these
Counsel's a Siren: if the leader list,
Wreck follows. Errant paths, straightly pursued,
Soon reach the goal; while wiser, well-thought ways
Wander about for fear of miry shoes.
And shall I hear one rasher than myself,
When wisdom would be folly!—Isabella,
A little way together, then farewell.—
[To **FORESTER**]
Friend, go before us.—Follow close. No word
Above a whisper.

ISABELLA
Must I leave you then?
Why are we made so that we trust our hopes!

[All go out.

ACT V

SCENE I.—A Passage in Berwick Castle

Enter **CROMBE** as jailor, carrying food. He opens a door, and the **COUNTESS OF BUCHAN** is discovered in a cage.

COUNTESS OF BUCHAN [Aside]
O me! Another! I can court no more.
This one I'll take by storm.—Fellow, good friend,
I think you are my thousandth jailor.
Soon I'll have a fresh one doubtless every day.
I've here had trial of my power on men,
On common vulgar men like you—for you
Are like your predecessors, I suppose—
And find myself most potent. Listen, now!
Yes, but you shall, you must; and look as well:
For I have looks like golden lightning, swift,
Gentle and perilous, that fascinate
The worshipful beholder. I have words,
Sweet words, soft words, and words like two-edged swords,
Like singing winds that rock the sense asleep,
Like waves full-breasted, filling deepest souls;
And I will kill you in a thousand ways
With words and looks unless you yield you now.
The others all were conquered just too late;
The women tell me nothing—English all;
But you will tell me what I want to know,
In brave submission to my witchery;
Now, like a man: I hope you are a man.

CROMBE
What must I tell you?

COUNTESS OF BUCHAN
You must tell me first
How the king is—King Robert Bruce, I mean.

CROMBE
They say he's well.

COUNTESS OF BUCHAN
Where is he then? But, sir,
I see you better now; you have an eye,
A brow, a mouth. Without more question, say
How Scotland fares since I was prisoned here.

CROMBE
Because of this same eye, and brow, and mouth
They made me jailor.

COUNTESS OF BUCHAN

O, I understand!
And being nobler than those stolid pikes—
Pike-handles, I should say—forerunning you,
You'll not do wrong in duty's name. Escape
You cannot help me to; but tell me, sir,
Some news.

CROMBE
Ah! Pardon me. If, as you say,
I have a brain to know that wrong is wrong
Though soldierly obedience be its badge,
Shall I not have the strength to overcome
Rebellious righteousness? Think you——

COUNTESS OF BUCHAN
James Crombe!

CROMBE
Your servant ever, lady.

COUNTESS OF BUCHAN
Pardon, friend;
I did not know you. I've no memory
Except for horrors. I am half a beast—
Starved, frozen, scorched, in rags. Sometimes at night
I'm mad. The rotten air, the subtle dark,
The clammy cold, crawl through my blood like worms:
They knot themselves in aches, they gnaw my flesh,
And I believe me dead. Ghosts visit me:
They come in undistinguishable throngs,
Sighing and moaning like a windy wood.
Demons invade my grave with flaming eyes,
With lolling tongues; and ugly horrors steam
And whirl about me. Mountains topple down,
Grazing my head; and threatening worlds approach,
But never whelm me. O my friend! O me!
Tell me for mercy's sake of living men!
How came you here?

CROMBE
To be beside you, lady.

COUNTESS OF BUCHAN
What! You are weeping! Dear friend, speak to me.
What food is this? White bread, and wine, and meat!
[Clapping her hands]
Thanks, thanks! O thanks! I'll eat, while you recount
All, all, about my friends!

CROMBE
My time is brief.
And first I'll tell you of an enemy.
Edward the First is dead.

COUNTESS OF BUCHAN
Say you! Aha!
That was a mighty villain.

CROMBE
Nigel is dead:
They killed him when they took Kildrummie tower.

COUNTESS OF BUCHAN
Ah, what a wanton waste of noble blood!
Remorseless tigers! Ah, the wolves, the rats!—
The queen, and Lady Douglas?

CROMBE
Prisoners both.

COUNTESS OF BUCHAN
The man, my husband?

CROMBE
Beaten, decayed, forgot.
When we were scattered in the wood of Drome,
The king sought refuge in an Irish isle,
Which in the spring he left, and dared his fate.
So after perils, and trials, and mighty acts,
And deeds of marvellous device—well poised
By those achievements, rare and manifold,
Heroically wrought by Edward Bruce,
Douglas, Boyd, Fraser, Gilbert de la Haye,
Randolf, and many another famous knight,
Whose deeds already ring in lands afar—
At Inverury he and your husband met:
And there the earl suffered such dread defeat,
That ignominy has become the grave
Where all his hopes lie buried.

COUNTESS OF BUCHAN
Wretched soul!

CROMBE
Now in the length and breadth of this free land,
One castle only is in England's power.

Would I had time to tell you how 'twas done!

COUNTESS OF BUCHAN
What castle?

CROMBE
Stirling. Edward found the siege
For his hot blood too long, and made a pact,
That if the governor, Sir Philip Mowbray,
Were not relieved within a year and day,
He should surrender. In the interval
Sir Philip went to London to the king—
Edward the Second, an unstable man—
And couched his eyes of that security
That curtained Scotland's state. He levied soon
The mightiest army ever England raised;
And in the sight of Stirling, Bruce and he
Are met to fight.

COUNTESS OF BUCHAN
Now?

CROMBE
Now. And news is come
That Bruce to-day o'erthrew a champion
Between the armies; and that Randolf fought
And conquered Clifford, who had dreadful odds.

COUNTESS OF BUCHAN
And are they fighting now?

CROMBE
No; but to-morrow
The battle is.

COUNTESS OF BUCHAN
Then, gallant friend, away!
Take horse and ride! You must not miss to-morrow.
Spur through the night!—Nay, think no more of me!
Or think me sitting lightsome on the croup,
And smiling at the moon. I go with you:
My soul is in your arm!—You must not stay.
One stout heart more!—Ride, ride!—I thank you, friend:
To know your dear and steadfast constancy,
As now I do, is worth these lonely years.—
Away to victory!—I can weep at last!—
Here, take this withered rag! It is the scarf
The queen gave me that far-off night in Drome.

My parched and desert eyes that sorrow shrunk
Are wet with happiness! See! Am I red?
My pale and stagnant blood wakes up again,
I would that we were flying together, Crombe,
As once we did, rebels, so free and glad!
Now go! Now go!—Yes, kiss me through the bars:
My kiss shall help to win the battle. Go!

[He kisses her, and goes out. The scene closes.

SCENE II.—The Scottish Camp at Bannockburn

BRUCE in his tent at night.

BRUCE
This drowned and abject mood; this sodden brain;
This broken back; this dull insanity,
That mopes and broods and has no thought at all;
This dross, that, in exchange for molten gold
Of madness thrice refined, were hell for heaven;
This flabby babe; this hare; this living death;
This sooty-hued, cold-blooded melancholy!
We know it for a subtle, potent lie—
A vapour, a mere mood! But when it comes,
Stealing upon us like unwelcome sleep
In high festivity, we've no more power
To shake our souls alive, than if we'd drunk
Of Lapland philtres,—muddy brew of hell!
When we, like beakers brimmed with wine, are full
Of living in the hand of God, there strikes
Some new divine idea through His brain,
And in the careless instant we are spilled
To be replenished never: so we feel.
We feel? How hard it is to fix the mind!
Only less hard than to withdraw it. Sleep?
No; not to-night. Heart, faithless heart, grow strong.
Ay, now I have remembrance of a thought
A dear breath whispered making wisdom sweet.
"Husband," she said, "when faith is strong in you,
Then only have you any right to think,
To judge, to act." And kissed me then, as if
Her healing truth had need of honey!
O, Love with its simple glance can pierce the night,
When drowsy sages at their tapers nod!
I will not trust myself but when self-trust
Is buoyant in me. And I surely know

to-morrow's battle finds one soul sufficient.—
I wonder how my wife is! Have these years,
These days, these hours—it is the hours that tell—
Dealt kindly with her in her nunnery?
Poor lady! She is gentle, delicate—
A lute that can respond to nothing harsh.
If she be shattered by this heavy stroke
Of separation! I, with sinewy strings,
Endure the constant quivering——

[Enter **GUARD**.

What now?

GUARD
The leaders wait without, your majesty.

BRUCE
Is it that time? Well, bid them enter.

[Enter **EDWARD BRUCE**, **DOUGLAS**, **RANDOLF**, and **WALTER** the Steward.

Friends,
Good morning. Let me see your eyes.—Randolf,
You have not slept.—Sir James, perhaps you have!
Your eyes were never dull.—What, half awake!
Why, Walter, love, if not anxiety,
Should have kept watch in that young head of yours!
Brother, I know you slept.

EDWARD BRUCE
Why should I not?
I thanked God for the error that I made
In giving respite to the garrison,
Since it has brought us to this desperate pass
Where we must conquer. Then I slept, and dreamt;
And wakened, laughing at I know not what.

RANDOLF
I had no sleep. This would not leave my mind,
That we were one to five.

BRUCE
Why Randolf, shame!
You are the last who should complain of that.
What good knight was it, like a water-drop,
Lost shape and being in an English sea,
Which found him out a rock, but yesterday?

Why man, you are my cousin, Thomas Randolf;
And this is Douglas; this, my brother Edward;
We are men who have done deeds, God helping us.
God helping us, we'll do a deed to-day!

RANDOLF
I do not fear; but, lonely, in the night
I could not see how we must win.

BRUCE
No! come.
[They go to the door of the tent and look out.
I see the battle as it will be fought.
The sun climbs up behind us: if he shine,
His beams will strike on English eyes. Look there!
The earth throws off her mourning nightly weed;
And the fresh dawn, her bowermaid, coyly comes
To veil her with the morning, like a bride
Worthy the sun's embrace. This fight you dread,
Regard it as a happy tournament
Played at the marriage of the fragrant world,
If the full weight and awe of its intent
Press on you too o'erwhelmingly.

RANDOLF
Not I.
I'd rather lose the fight for what it is,
Than win it jestingly.

BRUCE
Well said! The night,
That filled you with its gloom, out of your blood
Exhales, and it is day. Imagine, now:
Between high Stirling and the Bannock stream,
Whose silvery streak hot blood will tarnish soon,
Four battles stand. To westward, Edward's charge,
Douglas and Walter to the north and east,
Randolf, the doubter, in the central van;
I keep the second ward. Pent in this space
We cannot be unflanked, the river's gorge
On this wing, and on that, calthrops and pits.
The English archers scattered—Edward's task—
There but remains to stand, while yonder host,
Which leaves its revel only now, shall twine,
And knot, entangled in its proper coils,
Crammed in a cage too small for such a bulk,
Such sinuous length, such strength, to bustle in,
Save to its own confusion and dismay.

Speak I not reasonably, and quietly?

RANDOLF
Too quietly for me! Why, in this trap,
This coffin, they shall die for want of air!

EDWARD BRUCE
It is too cheap a victory!

DOUGLAS
When won,
I hope we may not find it all too dear.

[Bagpipes, drums, trumpets.

BRUCE
Ha! now the din begins! My blood is lit!
Come, let us set our soldiers in a glow!
After the abbot says the battle mass,
I'll speak to them, and touch them with a flame.

DOUGLAS
They'll burn.

EDWARD BRUCE
They'll make a bonfire.

WALTER the STEWARD
To announce
That Scotland's liberty's of age.

BRUCE
Well roared,
My lioncel!

[They go out.

SCENE III.—The Field of Bannockburn

Enter **EDWARD II**, the **EARL OF PEMBROKE**, **SIR GILES DE ARGENTINE**, **SIR INGRAM DE UMFRAVILLA**, with other **LORDS** and **KNIGHTS**, in advance of the English lines.

EDWARD II
Will yon men fight?

UMFRAVILLE

Ay, siccarly. My liege,
If you will hear an old man's humble word
Who knows the Scotchmen well, feign a retreat:
Then will these fiery children of the North—
Children they are in every gift save strength,
And most in guileless daring—rush on us,
Leaving their vantage, and be overcome
Utterly, as in many a fight before.

EDWARD II

I'm a young warrior, and I mean to win
By dint of strength, and not by strategy.
To sneak a victory I came not north;
But in a lordly way to overthrow
The base usurper of my lordship here.
Leave paltry sleights and fawnings upon chance
To starveling rebels, keen as hungry curs
That dodge the whip, and steal the bone at once.
Think you we brought our friends across the sea
To juggle with them? We are here to fight,
As in the lists, like gentlemen. My lords,
I give you Scotland. Nothing for myself
Save sovereignty I claim: and that must be
Not snared by ambush, for assassins fit,
But seized by courage, frank and English.

PEMBROKE

Sire,
One reason only urges strategy:
Adopting it, less English blood will flow.

EDWARD II

That touches me.

DE ARGENTINE

And it is kindly thought.
But I have heard the Scotsmen plume themselves
On victory over any English odds,
In battles, pitched, embroiled, and hand to hand;
That we have never vanquished them in fight
Except when treachery assisted arms.
Conquest unchallengeable, dearly bought
Were worth its cost. A wily victory
Would leave our foes unhumbled, unappeased,
And confident of ultimate success.

EDWARD II

This is the wisest counsel.

UMFRAVILLE

Hear me yet.
What warrior is wilier than Bruce?
The schiltron he has perfected: no knights
Can break the Scottish spearmen: chivalry
Means nought for them save mounted foes whose trust
Is in their horses——

EDWARD II

'Tis a base device,
This slaughter of our steeds! A dastard's trick!
The delicate art of war, where excellence
Lay in the power of noble blood alone,
He makes a trade for ploughmen. Battle-fields
Are shambles since this rebel taught his clowns
To fear not knighthood!

UMFRAVILLE

True indeed, my liege!
And some have thought that this new style of war
Will drive the other out. But see you not
That every possible advantage——

EDWARD II

No!
For I will not!—Behold, the Scots ask mercy!

UMFRAVILLE

They do—from Heaven. These men will win or die.

EDWARD II

I hate such kneeling, whining warriors, I!
What right have they to think God on their side?
Our glorious father taught them otherwise
With iteration one had deemed enough.
I burn to teach them finally. My lords,
Our swords shall pray for us. One hour's hot work,
And Scotland is your own. Let us begin!
Each to his post, and everlasting shame
Blight him who cherishes a moment's thought
Of other means of victory than these,
Our English bows and lances, English hearts,
And not less English courage of our friends
Whose foreign banners grace our army. Come;
England shall stretch from Orkney to Land's End
After to-day. St. George for Merry England!

[They go out.

Enter **BRUCE** and the other **LEADERS**.

BRUCE
I think we all know well what courage is:
Not thews, not blood, not bulk, not bravery:
Its highest title, patience. Fiery haste
Has lost most battles. Till the word be given,
Let no man charge to-day: no seeming flight
Must lead you to pursue: take root; grow strong;
The earth is Scottish. For our country stand
Like bastioned, frowning rocks that beard the sea,
And triumph everlastingly. Doubt not
The time to charge will come—once and straight home:
We'll need no spur: so must you curb your blood;
Command your anguished strength: a false start now
Will lose a race we cannot run again.
If any of you feel unfit for fight
From any cause whatever, let him go,
Leaving us undiluted. Scorn nor curse
Shall blast him; but our generous thought shall praise
His act and consecrate his name,
As one who did his best in doing nought;
For victory depends on each of us.
I say, if gallant souls be timorous,
Get them behind the hill, and be not sad:
Great courage goes to make an open coward.

[A great shout.

Then are we all one heart. Our enemies,
Our English enemies, who hope to drown
The very name of Scot in Scottish blood,
And these outlandish battle-harlots, hired
From Holland, Zealand, Brabant, Normandy,
Those Picards, Flemings, Gascons, Guiennese,
The refuse of the realms from which they swarm,
Are robbers lured by plunder, one and all,
From king to scullion: they are in the wrong.
We are the weapon to defend the right
God grasps to-day. Can we be put to shame?

SOLDIERS

No!

BRUCE
Forward, trusty friends! The hour is come
For long-desired redemption of the vows
Groaned out when tender mothers, sisters, wives,
Fathers we worshipped, brothers we adored,
Were spared not. Let our battle-cry be—No;
I'll give you none. Each soldier shout the name
Of that best friend in prison buried quick;
Of yonder heaven-homed, most beloved soul
Among the multitude whose butchered limbs
Lie pledged in sepulchres. My countrymen,
Welcome to victory, which must be ours,
For death is freedom!

SOLDIERS
Victory or death!

[Exeunt.

SCENE V.—The Gillies' Hill

MEN and **WOMEN** watching the battle.

A YOUNG FRIAR
"St. Andrew and St. George! Fight on! fight on!"
A whole year's storms let loose on one small lake
Prisoned among the mountains, rioting
Between the heathery slopes and rugged cliffs,
Dragging the water from its deepest lair,
Shaking it out like feathers on the blast;
With shock on shock of thunder; shower on shower
Of jagged and sultry lightning; banners, crests,
Of rainbows torn and streaming, tossed and flung
From panting surge to surge; where one strong sound,
Enduring with continuous piercing shriek
Whose pitch is ever heightened, still escapes
Wroth from the roaring war of elements;
Where mass and motion, flash and colour spin
Wrapped and confounded in their blent array:
And this all raving on a summer's morn,
With unseen larks beside the golden sun,
And merest blue above; with not a breeze
To fan the burdened rose-trees, or incense
With mimic rage the foamless rivulet,

That like a little child goes whispering
Along the woodland ways its happy thought;
Were no more wild, grotesque, fantastical,
Uncouth, unnatural—and I would think
Impossible, but for the vision here—
Than is this clamorous and unsightly war,
Where swords and lances, shields and arrows, flash,
Whistle, and clang—splintered like icicles,
Eclipsed like moons, broken like reeds, like flames—
Lewd flames that lick themselves in burning lust—
With scorpion tongues lapping the lives of men;
Where axes cut to hearts worth all the oaks;
Where steel burns blue, and golden armours blaze—
One moment so, the next, a ruddier hue;
Where broidered banners rustle in the charge,
And deck the carnage out—A skeleton,
Ribboned and garlanded may sweetly suit
The morris-dancers for a May-pole now!—
Where hoofs of horses spatter brains of men,
And beat dull thunder from the shaking sod;
Where yelling pibrochs, braying trumpets, drums,
And shouts, and shrieks, and groans, hoarse, shrill—a roar
That shatters hearing—echo to the sky;
Where myriad ruthless vessels, freighted full
Of proud rich blood—with images of God,
Their reasoning souls, deposed from their command—
By winds of cruel hate usurped and urged,
Are driven upon each other, split, and wrecked,
And foundered deep as hell. The air is dark
With souls. I cannot look—I cannot see.

[Kneels.

A WOMAN
The battle's lost before it's well begun.
Our men fall down in ranks like barley-rigs
Before a dense wet blast.

A CRIPPLE
Despair itself
Can only die before the English bows.
O that they could come at them! Who are these
That skirt the marsh?

WOMAN
My sight is weak. But see;
Here's an old fellow, trembling, muttering. Look
How he is strung; and what an eye he has!

CRIPPLE

Old sight sees well away. I warrant, now,
His is a perfect mirror of the fight.
You see well, father?

OLD MAN

Ay. That's Edward Bruce;
And none too soon. The feathered deaths speed thick
In jubilant choirs, flight after singing flight:
That tune must end; the nest be harried. Ride,
Fiery Edward! Yet our staunch hearts quail not.
Ah! now the daze begins! I know it well.
The cloth-yard shafts like magic shuttles, weave
Athwart the warped air dazzling, dire dismay,
And the beholder's blood slinks to his heart
Like moles from daylight; all his sinews fade
To unsubstantial tinder. Ha! spur! spur!
There are ten thousand bowmen! Gallop! Charge!
Now, by the soul of Wallace, Edward Bruce,
The battle's balanced! On your sword it hangs!
Look you; there's fighting! Just a minute's fight!
Tug, strain! Throe upon throe! Travail of war!
The birth—defeat and victory, those twins,
That in an instant breathe and die, and leave
So glorious and so dread a memory!—
The bowstring's cut! What butchery to see!
They shear them down, these English yeomen! God!
It looks like child's play too! And so it feels,
Now I remember me.—That's victory.
St. Andrew and the right!

WOMAN

The knights, the knights!

OLD MAN

I see them. But our spearmen! Do you see?
This hill we stand on trembles with the shock:
They budge not, planted, founded in the soil.
Another charge! Now watch! Now see! Ugh! Ha!
Did one spear flicker? One limb waver? No!
These fellows there are fighting for their land!
The English army through its cumbrous bulk
Thrilled and astounded to the utmost rear,
Twists like a snake, and folds into itself,
Rank pushed through rank. Now are they hand to hand!
How short a front! How close! They're sewn together
With steel cross-stitches, halbert over sword,

Spear across lance, and death the purfled seam!
I never saw so fierce, so locked a fight!
That tireless brand that like a pliant flail
Threshes the lives from sheaves of Englishmen—
Know you who wields it? Douglas, who but he!
A noble meets him now. Clifford it is!
No bitterer foes seek out each other there.
Parried! That told! and that! Clifford, good night!
And Douglas shouts to Randolf; Edward Bruce
Cheers on the Steward; while the King's voice rings
In every Scotch ear: such a narrow strait
Confines this firth of war!

YOUNG FRIAR
God gives me strength
Again to gaze with eyes unseared. Jewels!
These must be jewels peering in the grass,
Cloven from helms, or on them: dead men's eyes
Scarce shine so bright. The banners dip and mount
Like masts at sea. The battle-field is slime,
A ruddy lather beaten up with blood!
Men slip; and horses, stuck with shafts like butts,
Sprawl, madly shrieking! No, I cannot look!

[Exit.

WOMAN
Look here! look here, I say! Who's this behind?
His horse sinks down—the brute is dead, I think.
His clothes are torn; his face with dust and sweat
Encrusted, baked, and cracked. He speaks; he shouts;
And shouting runs this way. He's mad, I think.

CRIPPLE
He's made his hearers mad. Tents, blankets, poles,
Pitch-forks, and staves, and knives, brandished and spread
By women, children, grandsires! What is this?

[Enter **CROMBE** followed by a **CROWD** bearing blankets for banners, and armed with staves, etc.

CROMBE
I rode all night to strike a blow to-day:
The noblest lady living bade me go:
Her kiss is on my lips and in my soul.
Come after me—yea, with your naked hands,
And conquer weapons!

[They go out, shouting.

To them enter **BRUCE**.

BRUCE
Most noble souls who wait so patiently!
Your splendid faith is in the air about you;
Your steady eyes shine like a galaxy;
Your presence comforts me: pressed in the fight,
The thought of you, like balm upon a wound,
Softened the thriftless aching of my heart.
The English waver; on the hill behind
Our followers fright them, marching in array
Bannered and armed, a legion out of heaven.
The tide of battle turns, and victory
Needs only you to launch it bravely forth.
Now—I would bid you think, but that the thought
Eludes me, like a homely, old-known song,
Wreathing in fitful gusts beyond the sense—
Now will the lofty keystone of our life
Be pitched in heaven for ever. We have dreamt
Our prayers into fulfilment many a time:
to-day we wrestle, and the victory's ours:
And yet I feel so scantly what it means
That I'm ashamed. Enough: I know you all.—
Now for our homes, our children, and our wives,
For freedom, for our land, for victory!
And cry our old cry, Carrick!

SOLDIERS
Carrick and victory!

[They go out.

John Davidson – A Short Biography

John Davidson was born at Barrhead, East Renfrewshire on 11th April 1857, the son of Alexander Davidson, an Evangelical Union minister and Helen née Crocket of Elgin.

In 1862 the family moved to Greenock and Davidson began his education at Highlanders' Academy. From there he began his career, aged a mere 13, at the chemical laboratory of Walker's Sugarhouse refinery. A year later he returned to Highlander's, this time as a pupil teacher.

During his later employment at the Public Analysts' Office, 1870–71 he developed a keen interest in science which later became an important characteristic of his poetry. He returned once again to the Highlander's Academy, this time for four years, in 1872, again as a pupil teacher. In 1876 he spent a year at Edinburgh University before his first scholastic employment at Alexander's Charity, Glasgow which led to short periods of employment at various other schools over the following half a dozen years.

This led to a stint at Morrison's Academy in Crieff (1885–88), and in a private school at Greenock (1888–89).

In 1885 Davidson married Margaret McArthur and the marriage produced two children, Alexander (born in 1887) and Menzies (born in 1889).

Davidson's first published work was 'Bruce, A Chronicle Play', written in the Elizabethan style, and published by a local Glasgow imprint in 1886. Four other plays quickly followed; 'Smith, A Tragic Farce' (1888), 'An Unhistorical Pastoral' (1889), 'A Romantic Farce' (1889), and then the somewhat brilliant pantomime 'Scaramouch in Naxos' (1889).

By now he was very much immersed in literature and, in 1889, he ventured to London where he frequented the famous Fleet Street pub 'Ye Olde Cheshire Cheese' and joined the 'Rhymers' Club', a poets group that was based there.

Davidson was a prolific and hard-working writer. As well as his plays he wrote for the Speaker, the Glasgow Herald, and several other papers. He also wrote and had published several novels and tales, with perhaps the best being 'Perfervid' (1890).

With his reputation gradually providing an income he was also able to explore his true medium; Verse. 'In a Music Hall and Other Poems' (1891) together with 'Fleet Street Eclogues' (1893) were ample proof that he possessed a quite rare, genuine and distinctive poetic gift. Praise came from his peers including George Gissing and WB Yeats who wrote that it was: 'An example of a new writer seeking out new subject matter, new emotions'.

Davidson now turned further and further towards verse. In 1894 he published his most popular volume, 'Ballads and Songs' (1894), and this was followed by a further 'Fleet Street Eclogues' (Second Series) (1896) and by 'New Ballads' (1897) and 'The Last Ballad' (1899).

Davidson was a prolific writer. Besides the works cited, he wrote many other works including, 'The Wonderful Mission of Earl Lavender' (1895), a novel which extends his literary canon to flagellation erotica. He also contributed an introduction to Shakespeare's Sonnets (Renaissance edition, 1908), which, like his various prefaces and essays, shows him to be a subtle literary critic.

As the new century dawned Davidson was hard at work on a series of 'Testaments', in which he gave definite expression to his philosophy and these were published over a seven year period; 'The Testament of a Vivisector' (1901), 'The Testament of a Man Forbid' (1901), 'The Testament of an Empire Builder' (1902), and 'The Testament of John Davidson' (1908).

Though he played down any thought of himself as a philosopher, he expounded an original philosophy which was at once materialistic and aristocratic.

His later verse, which is often fine rhetoric rather than poetry, expressed his belief which is summed up in the last words that he wrote, "Men are the universe become conscious; the simplest man should consider himself too great to be called after any name." Davidson professed to reject all existing philosophies, including that of Nietzsche, as inadequate. The poet planned to expand and expound on his revolutionary creed in a trilogy entitled 'God and Mammon'. Only two plays, however, were written, 'The Triumph of Mammon' (1907) and 'Mammon and his Message' (1908).

In addition to his own work Davidson was a noted translator of other works which included Montesquieu's 'Lettres Persanes' (1892), François Coppée's 'Pour la Couronne' in 1896 and Victor Hugo's 'Ruy Blas' in 1904, the former being produced as, 'For the Crown', at the Lyceum Theatre in 1896, the latter as 'A Queen's Romance' at the Imperial Theatre.

Frank Harris, a member of the Rhymers' Club and himself a writer of erotic literature described him in 1889 as: "... a little below middle height, but strongly built with square shoulders and remarkably fine face and head; the features were almost classically regular, the eyes dark brown and large, the forehead high, the hair and moustache black. His manners were perfectly frank and natural; he met everyone in the same unaffected kindly human way; I never saw a trace in him of snobbishness or incivility. Possibly a great man, I said to myself, certainly a man of genius, for simplicity of manner alone is in England almost a proof of extraordinary endowment."

In 1906 he was awarded a civil list pension of £100 per annum and George Bernard Shaw did what he could to help him financially. However other issues were also circling besides poverty. Ill-health, and his declining intellectual powers, amplified by the onset of cancer, caused profound hopelessness and clinical depression.

Late in 1908, Davidson left London to live in Penzance in Cornwall. On 23rd March 1909, he left his house and was not seen again. There seemed no sound reason not to believe that he had done so with the intention of drowning himself. On an examination of his office a new manuscript was found. It was a poetry book; 'Fleet Street Poems', with a letter bleakly stating confirming, "This will be my last book."

Indeed in his philosophic book 'The Testament of John Davidson', published the year before his death, he anticipates this fate:

"None should outlive his power. . . . Who kills
Himself subdues the conqueror of kings;
Exempt from death is he who takes his life;
My time has come."

Davidson's body was not discovered until 18th September in Mount's cave by some fishermen. In accordance with his will it was now buried at sea. Strangely it seemed Davidson's wish that none of his unpublished works, nor any biography be published and "no word except of my writing is ever to appear in any book of mine as long as the copyright endures."

Davidson's poetry was a key early influence on important Modernist poets, in particular, his compatriot Hugh MacDiarmid, Wallace Stevens and T.S. Eliot.

The North Wall (1885)
Diabolus Amans (1885) Verse drama
Bruce (1886) A drama in five acts
Smith (1888) A tragedy
An Unhistorical Pastoral, A Romantic Farce (1889)
Scaramouch in Naxos (1889)
Perfervid: The Career of Ninian Jamieson (1890) with 23 Original Illustrations by Harry Furniss
The Great Men, And a Practical Novelist (1891) Illustrated by E. J. Ellis.
In a Music Hall, and other Poems (1891)
Laura Ruthven's Widowhood (with C. J. Wills) (1892)
Fleet Street Eclogues (1893)
The Knight of the Maypole, (1903)
Sentences and Paragraphs (1893)
Ballads and Songs (1894)
Baptist Lake (1894)
A Random Itinerary (1894)
A Full and True Account of the Wonderful Mission of Earl Lavender (1895)
St. George's Day (1895)
Fleet Street Eclogues (Second Series) (1896)
Miss Armstrong's and Other Circumstances (1896)
The Pilgrimage of Strongsoul and Other Stories (1896)
New Ballads (1897)
Godfrida, a play (1898)
The Last Ballad (1899)
Self's the Man, A tragi-comedy (1901)
The Testament of a Man Forbid (1901)
The Testament of a Vivisector (1901)
The Testament of an Empire Builder (1902)
A Rosary (1903)
The Knight of the Maypole: A Comedy in Four Acts (1903)
The Testament of a Prime Minister (1904)
The Ballad of a Nun (1905)
The Theatrocrat: A Tragic Play of Church and State (1905)
Holiday and other poems, with a note on poetry (1906)
The Triumph of Mammon (1907)
Mammon and His Message (1908)
The Testament of John Davidson (1908)
Fleet Street and other Poems (1909)

He was also a contributor to 'The Yellow Book' periodical

As Translator

Montesquieu's Lettres Persanes (Persian Letters) (1892)
François Coppée's Pour la couronne (For the Crown) (1896)

Victor Hugo's Ruy Blas (A Queen's Romance) (1904)